Praise for *Screen*

ens, think
e, this book

Kevin Leman | *New York Times* bestselling author of *Why Your Kids Misbehave and What to Do about It* and *Making Children Mind without Losing Yours*

In *Screen Kids,* Chapman and Pellicane teach the relationship skills children need to learn because of technology's negative influence over them. Technology has been here long enough that we know the decline in social skills is causing children to be miserable, lonely, confused, angry, misled, depressed, and unfulfilled. The truths on these pages will equip children for life, school, family time, and quality relationships. You and they will make realistic and significant changes so they willingly decrease their screen time and confidently increase their friend time.

Kathy Koch | Founder and president of Celebrate Kids, Inc., and author of *Five to Thrive, 8 Great Smarts,* and *Screens and Teens*

During this past century, great advances have been made, and none more amazing than mankind's ability to communicate in this computer generation. We have abilities beyond anything ever imagined, but there are also real challenges for kids whose time, thoughts, and direction are being consumed. Arlene Pellicane and Gary Chapman have filled the pages of this book with words of understanding, instruction, caution, and advice for parents. It's a never-ending flow of information. This book is a must-read!

Mel Cheatham | Clinical Professor of Neurosurgery, UCLA David Geffen School of Medicine

I believe that screens are the most significant contributor to a growing epi-demic of anxiety and depression in our children. *Screen Kids* is one of the books I most recommend to parents as a must-read. And the book is provided by two of the most trusted voices in parenting and family relationships—Gary Chapman and Arlene Pellicane. Please, I beg you, read this book!

Dannah Gresh | Bestselling author of *Lies Girls Believe* and founder of True Girl

This book will help parents navigate the slippery slope of electronics in a way that emphasizes family bonding, social relating, and maintaining a healthy balance of electronic and nonelectronic activities. A most welcome addition to the library of any intentional parent.

Todd Cartmell | Child psychologist and author of *Project Dad* and *Raising Flexible Kids*

As a mom, I have often felt outnumbered in my own home: laptop, iPod, smartphone, Xbox, tablet: 5 vs. Mom and Dad: 2. Besides living in a wireless bunker, what's a parent to do? *Screen Kids* will help you reclaim your home and your family. More than a media manifesto, this book shares a commonsense, real-world approach to building relationships and helping our kids who are screen savvy become socially savvy.

Kathi Lipp | Bestselling author of *The Husband Project*, *Clutter Free*, and *Ready for Anything*

In this unprecedented age of technology and its accessibility, I cannot think of a more needed or more important resource for parents than *Screen Kids*. While this book recognizes the positive contributions of technology, it serves as an important handbook for educating parents on the effects of too much screen time in our lives. It offers creative alternatives and encouragement to take back our home from the digital invasion, and I highly recommend it!

Kristen Welch | Author of *Raising Grateful Kids in an Entitled World*; blogger at We Are THAT Family

Finally, a book that educates parents on the very real effects "screen time" has on our children and daily home life. *Screen Kids* is packed with practical wisdom and brilliant suggestions to effectively and intentionally pull families trapped in isolation away from their screens to reestablish God-intended family time! Gary and Arlene, count me a raving fan of this much-needed guidebook for parents!

Tracey Eyster | Founder of FamilyLife's MomLifeToday.com and author of *Be the Mom* and *Beautiful Mess*

As a mom of ten children, I see now more than ever how important real connections with real people are. Thankfully, Arlene Pellicane and Dr. Gary Chapman have provided sound advice for parents in how to train children in important relational skills, while setting realistic boundaries for electronic entertainment. Need help in teaching your children communication, care, and empathy for others? This is the book you've been looking for! Great research, sound advice, and steps to success—what could be better than that?

Tricia Goyer | *USA Today* bestselling author of seventy-five books, including *Lead Your Family Like Jesus*

Screen Kids is a must-read for wisdom to maximize the positives and minimize the negatives of life and love in the ever-changing digital world.

Pam and Bill Farrel | Codirectors of Love-Wise; authors of thirty-eight books

5 RELATIONAL SKILLS EVERY CHILD NEEDS IN A TECH-DRIVEN WORLD

Screen Kids

GARY CHAPMAN
AND ARLENE PELLICANE

NORTHFIELD PUBLISHING
CHICAGO

This book was previously published as *Growing Up Social: Raising Relational Kids in a Screen-Driven World* (2014).

Some names have been changed to protect the privacy of individuals.

Edited by Elizabeth Cody Newenhuyse
Interior and cover design: Erik M. Peterson
Cover illustration of cardboard phone copyright © 2019 by Marie Maerz/Adobe Stock (105871809).
Cover illustrations of people copyright © 2018 by Sudowoodo /iStock (1057675582).
All rights reserved for the above illustrations.
Chapman Photo Credit: P.S.Photography
Pellicane Photo credit:Anthony Amorteguy

Library of Congress Cataloging-in-Publication Data

Names: Chapman, Gary D., 1938- author. | Pellicane, Arlene, 1971- author.
Title: Screen kids : 5 relational skills every child needs in a tech-driven world / Gary Chapman and Arlene Pellicane.
Description: Chicago : Northfield Publishing, [2020] | Includes bibliographical references. | Summary: "Today, children spend more time interacting with screens and less time playing outside or interacting with family. Screen Kids will empower you to make positive changes. This newly revised edition features the latest research and interactive assessments, so you can best confront the issues technology creates in your home"-- Provided by publisher.
Identifiers: LCCN 2020020567 (print) | LCCN 2020020568 (ebook) | ISBN 9780802422200 (paperback) | ISBN 9780802499035 (ebook)
Subjects: LCSH: Technology and children. | Internet and children. | Internet addiction in adolescence. | Interpersonal relations in children.
Classification: LCC HQ784.T37 C48 2020 (print) | LCC HQ784.T37 (ebook) | DDC 004.67/8083--dc23
LC record available at https://lccn.loc.gov/2020020567
LC ebook record available at https://lccn.loc.gov/2020020568

Northfield Publishing
820 N. LaSalle Boulevard
Chicago, IL 60610

1 3 5 7 9 10 8 6 4 2

Printed in the United States of America

CONTENTS

Authors' Note 7

Introduction 11

Part 1 • Kids on Tech

1. Screen Time and the Brain 23
2. Screen Time and Relationships 37
3. Screen Time and Safety 49
4. Screen Time and Emotional Health 65
5. Screen Time and the Single Parent 79

Part 2 • The A+ Social Skills

6. The A+ Skill of Affection 93
7. The A+ Skill of Appreciation 105
8. The A+ Skill of Anger Management 119
9. The A+ Skill of Apology 131
10. The A+ Skill of Attention 145

Part 3 • Restart Your Home

11. Screen Time and You 161
12. Top Ten Questions and Answers 173

Quiz: Does Your Child Have Too Much Screen Time? . . 183

Quiz: Is Your Child Addicted to Video Games? 185

Notes 187

About the Authors 201

Authors' Note

Significant new research has emerged since we published *Growing Up Social: Raising Relational Kids in a Screen-Driven World.* That's why we decided to update the book and retitle it *Screen Kids* to make it easier to find for a whole new tribe of parents. The National Institutes of Health has launched the largest-ever study of adolescent health and development. The Adolescent Brain Cognitive Development (ABCD) study will follow 11,874 children starting at ages nine and ten for the next decade.

Early findings reveal a link between screen time and a variety of complex structural brain changes.[1] We want you to be screen smart, knowing how these changes touch your children and our society.

The world now has more young people than ever before. Of the 7.2 billion people in the world, over 3 billion are younger than twenty-five. More than 1 billion of these young people are between ten and nineteen years old.[2] What is profoundly different about this group compared to generations past? In one word: technology.

Certainly the recent pandemic and the need for us all to isolate ourselves to reduce the spread of the virus has greatly increased the role of tech in all our lives. From Zoom family gatherings to online "school" to quick access to the latest news, we have seen the benefits of connectivity. However, the larger issue still remains: for our children, screen time is a double-edged sword.

In 2011, 52 percent of homes in the United States had a mobile device used by kids eight and under. By 2017, that number jumped to 98 percent of homes. From 2013 to 2017, mobile media time for kids eight and under has tripled.[3] Technology has benefited our lives in many ways, but it has also created a tsunami wave of 24/7 entertainment for which most parents are woefully unprepared. When Steve Jobs unveiled the revolutionary iPad in 2010, he persuaded millions to buy one. But when *New York Times* journalist Nick Bolton asked how his children were enjoying the popular new product, Jobs replied, "They haven't used it. We limit how much technology our kids use at home." Wait a minute. Hold the iPad. Steve Jobs didn't even let his own kids use one?

He's not the only tech insider to radically limit technology in the family. Bill and Melinda Gates banned cellphones for their kids before they turned fourteen. Evan Williams, founder of Blogger, Twitter, and Medium, bought hundreds of physical books for his two young sons but refused to get them an iPad.[4] Chris Anderson, former editor of *Wired* and father of five, did not allow iPads, calling them "gaming crack."[5] Many Silicon Valley executives are opting out of tech-savvy schools and choosing unwired classrooms with chalkboards instead.

Researchers in the ABCD study examined physical activity, screen time behavior, and sleep among more than 4,500 of the participants. They found that children who met these three daily recommendations had stronger attention, language abilities, working memory, and executive function:

At least sixty minutes of physical activity
No more than two hours of recreational screen time
Nine to eleven hours of sleep

These daily recommendations are a solid place to start. Unfortunately, only half of the children in the sample got the recommended amount of sleep, just 36 percent had fewer than two hours of screen time, and only 17 percent engaged in the recommended daily exercise.[6]

My (Arlene's) three children were elementary school age and younger when we wrote *Growing Up Social.* Now Ethan and Noelle are in high school, and Lucy is in middle school. We have practiced these three recommendations, and the principles in this book, and can testify they really do work.

When your child moves out of your home for college or a career, you're not going to say, "I wish I could go back in time and give my child more video game hours" or "I wish I would have given my child a phone and social media sooner." However, we have heard from many parents who have wished the opposite. They desperately wish for more time and memories with their children without the blinding distraction of the phone or tablet.

You don't have to leave your future to wishing. You can make a difference right now with your child. The experiences of many families in the recent stay-at-home period have, perhaps, reintroduced us to the joys of board games, puzzles, and playing in the yard. It isn't too late to disengage with devices and connect again to the ones you love most. It's our prayer this book will help you do just that.

And to stimulate further discussion, you can find questions related to this book—and your experiences—on *5lovelanguages .com.*

Gary Chapman, PhD
Winston-Salem, North Carolina

Arlene Pellicane, MA
San Diego, California

Introduction

Everybody now has a tablet or an iPhone or a smart device. . . .
That's how my career exploded.
—KIMBERLY YOUNG, FOUNDER,
CENTER FOR INTERNET ADDICTION

If you have kids, you can probably relate to Joseph and Amanda. They have three children, ages two, six, and ten. Their kids play video games and watch television most of the day except for the time the older kids are in school. Joseph and Amanda are very concerned about the amount of time their children spend in front of screens. Yet they feel helpless and powerless to make a change.

"We have no guidelines," said Joseph. "We did have guidelines, but could not keep them in place."

Can you identify with these discouraged parents? You've tried to limit screen time in the past, but the temper tantrums were too much to bear. We have heard from hundreds of parents who've expressed their frustration with implementing digital guidelines.

"Screen time rules aren't stated, they're implied, and it's not working."

"My kids know they only get one hour of screen time, but it's a constant battle."

"I regret not enforcing the rules, because my son missed out on socializing with people. He's in his twenties and completely engrossed with playing video games."

The training necessary for growing up with relational skills isn't found on a phone or tablet. No app or video game has been developed that can replace interaction with other human beings. Social skills must be practiced in real life, beginning for a child in the home where a loving mother or father can model what healthy relationships look like.

Unfortunately, there has been a subtle shift toward individual screen use that is profoundly eroding the relationship between parent and child. Kids age eight and under spend an average of two hours and nineteen minutes a day with screen media (with a dramatic shift to mobile devices).[1]

Teens spend seven hours and twenty-two minutes a day on screens, not including school or homework.[2] When we reminisce about the "good old days" before TikTok, endless streaming, and YouTube for little ones, it's really the togetherness we long for, not the nostalgia of a bygone era. There's no going back to the black-and-white, only-three-channels television of the 1950s—and most of us are grateful for that.

Technology gives our children access to all sorts of information, both good and bad. It is pretty amazing that your child can learn how to sketch a portrait, build a rocket, speak a different language, or video chat with someone who lives halfway around the world. As mentioned, during the recent pandemic, with parents *and* children forced to stay home, technology was a blessing for many families. And it is up to us as parents to guide our children to the positives of technology while minimizing risks.

This is no easy task. According to a Barna Group study, eight in ten parents (78%) believe it's more complicated today to raise children than in their parents' day, and 65 percent of the respondents blame technology and social media.[3]

We must begin this journey with a decision to put our children *before* our devices. It's time to treat our kids with more respect and attention than we give our phones. And we must fight for our kids to experience *childhood* before experiencing *devices*. A real childhood is filled with play, books, skinned knees, adventures, and imagination, not just sitting, swiping, and tapping. Although it may sound harsh, a phone is like a childhood killer. Once a child gets one, the door of childhood swiftly closes. Old hobbies and imaginary play are left behind for the intoxication of the digital world. Kids stop looking up and around at the world in curiosity—their heads go down and stay down.

WHY IT'S SO HARD TO STOP

Let's imagine you were waiting to board an airplane with your child, and the gate agent gave this warning: "Side effects of boarding today's flight may include obesity, mental health issues, sleep deprivation, social incompetence, attention problems, anxiety, depression, addictions, delayed speech and reading, motor deficits, eye damage, and musculoskeletal disorders."[4] Would you get on the flight? Probably not!

Yet the more time a child spends on a screen, the greater the risk for those life-altering side effects. We keep boarding the screen-time plane because it's convenient, everyone else seems to be on board, and frankly, we can't get our kids to stop jumping on. Douglas Gentile, psychology professor at Iowa State University, says, "It's been getting harder for parents to really monitor a lot of what their kids are seeing and doing. At the same time, they're relying on the seeming benefit of being able to quiet the kids at a restaurant with a device. . . . We may be building a bit of a Frankenstein's monster, because we're using that power for our benefit, not for the child's benefit."[5]

Powerful forces are at work to get you and your kids on screens as often as possible. The device in your child's chubby little hand (and yours) is not neutral. Former Google design ethicist Tristan Harris says the problem isn't that people lack willpower. It's that "there are a thousand people on the other side of the screen whose job it is to break down the self-regulation you have."[6] Phones and tablets are supercharged to engage your child on every possible level, designed to capture attention and never let go. In his book *Irresistible: The Rise of Addictive Technology and the Business of Keeping Us Hooked,* Adam Alter explains why it's so hard for kids and adults to disengage from screen time:

1. There are no stopping cues. Here's how television used to work: You watched your favorite program for thirty minutes, then the commercials came on (plus one break in the middle of the show). You didn't like the next show, so you turned off the TV or changed the channel. You had to wait a whole week to watch again. But now, when your son streams his favorite show, there are no stopping points. Nothing cues your son to think, "Oh, the program is over. I should do my homework or walk the dog now." Instead of a stopping point, another program (or the next episode) cues up automatically and starts playing. You understand this temptation because it happens to you as well!

Before Netflix introduced "post-play" in 2012, you had to *choose to watch* another episode. Now you have to *choose not to watch.* That little change has ushered in an age of binge-watching. YouTube works the same way, cueing up and playing the next recommended video. Decades ago you put a quarter into Ms. PacMan to play, and soon after (unless you were really good) it would say GAME OVER. No more. When a game ends today, it just starts again.[7]

Social media works the same way. You can scroll for hours and you will never find an end. It is bottomless. Unlike a physical newspaper, which has a front page and back page, social media goes on forever. Stopping cues have been eradicated. That's why you as a parent must provide the stopping cue. You can tell your child after one program, you will be coming to turn the screen off. You can set a timer for fifteen minutes, and when it beeps, it's time to stop checking social media or watching YouTube videos. Once you understand the bottomless nature of screens and how they are engineered to exploit our weaknesses, you can begin to fight back.

2. *Screens provide unpredictable rewards.* In 1971, a psychologist named Michael Zeiler conducted his now-famous experiment with pigeons about the best way to deliver rewards. Sometimes the pigeons would peck at a button, and a pellet would drop every time. Other times, the food was only delivered some of the time. The results revealed the pigeons pecked almost twice as often when the reward wasn't guaranteed. Their brains "were releasing far more dopamine when the reward was unexpected than when it was predictable."[8]

Like those pigeons, your child loves receiving unpredictable and intermittent rewards during screen time. If your daughter knew that every time she posted a photo, she would get exactly ten likes, that process would get boring for her. But if she posts a photo and has no idea how many likes she will get, now that's interesting! Posting on social is like pulling the lever on a slot machine—what kind of feedback will I get? Will my friends love it? Will they ignore it?

Video game designers know gamers are likely to stop playing a game that doesn't quickly deliver a dose of small, intermittent rewards. Those rewards could be as basic as a "ding" sound or a flash of light. Dr. Nick Yee studies how games affect players and says, "Rewards are given very quickly in the beginning of the game. You kill a creature with two to three hits. You gain a level in five to ten minutes. And you can gain crafting skill with very little failure. But the intervals between these rewards grow exponentially fairly quickly. Very soon, it takes five hours and then twenty hours of game time before you can gain a level. The game works by giving you instantaneous gratification upfront and leading you down a slippery slope."[9]

In real life, when your child eats green beans, fireworks don't go off above your dinner table. Riding your bike to school doesn't culminate in you earning a special badge. Dings and whistles don't sound when you complete your math homework. It can be hard for "real life" to compete with the electronic rewards of screen time.

3. *Screens tap into the power of goals.* Snapchat leveraged our innate desire to reach goals with the creation of the "streak." A streak means you and one of your Snapchat friends have both snapped each other a picture or video within a twenty-four-hour period for at least three consecutive days. The idea is that you and your friend keep this streak going for as long as possible. Some super goal-oriented Snapchatters have kept their streak going for more than 1,400 days. That's every day for almost four years!

When you have a streak going with a friend, a little fire emoji appears by your name along with the number of days you've successfully kept the streak going. Some kids, when they're trapped somewhere without Wi-Fi, worry about how they're going to keep that streak going. Screens are addictive because they tap into this power of goal setting.

These goals set by screens are usually artificial. If your girl meets her goal of having two hundred followers, does that really help her become a better friend? Did that accomplishment give her a sense of peace and well-being because she has close friends now? Probably not.

In video games, there is a well-defined goal. Save the princess, launch the bird, collect the treasures, shoot the enemy. The goals are measurable, and your child can see his score climb higher and higher. He might be able to crush it in a video game, but what about real-life goals? Depending on your child's age, these goals would be much more helpful to achieve:

- Do my own laundry
- Learn how to cook dinner
- Complete my homework without needing a reminder
- Practice the piano fifteen minutes a day
- Read one chapter of the Bible a day

Yet screen time doesn't usually promote these kinds of practical and developmental goals. On the contrary, screens *compete* with the completion of these goals. We must be mindful of the screen's ability to hijack good goals by giving your kids an artificial—and inferior—goal.

"I'M NOT CONCERNED": WHAT PARENTS THINK

Kids and teens aren't the only demographic prone to peer pressure. The other fourth-graders in your daughter's class have a phone, so you get her one too. If the other kids are playing a particular video game, even if you think it's too violent, what's the harm in your son joining in? You wouldn't want him to feel left out. Or maybe you feel bad about plunking your toddler in front of the screen for a few hours each day, but at least all the other kids you know are watching the same programs. One study reported 42 percent of kids eight and younger have their own tablet.[10] Between 2012 and 2018, teens owning mobile devices or tablets increased from 41 percent to 89 percent. Teens using social media several times a day increased from 34 percent to 70 percent.[11]

We surveyed hundreds of parents about their family and screens. Many of them reported that screens ran their children's life, yet they also reported they were not worried. One parent said, "My children can watch as much as they want, usually four or five hours a day. I'm not concerned and I don't think it's affected our family dynamic."

The presence of screens in the home is so widely accepted that many parents don't even consider them a threat to their children. Most schools are using laptops and iPads in the classroom to prepare students for work in the twenty-first century. Technology will be an integral part of your child's future workplace (just as it is with yours now).

Let us take a moment to assure you that this is not an anti-technology book. Technology is here to stay, and, as we have already observed, when rightly used, it offers a wealth of benefits. Society is increasingly structured around tech—think online shopping, rideshare apps, and so much more. But when it comes to children, to uncritically accept the dominance of tech . . . that's another story.

When your child has free time, what's their default activity? For the average family, free time equals screen time. Turning automatically to screens is going to become a habit for the rest of your child's life. Screen time that is not purposeful tends to be a waste of time and a negative influence. Malcolm Gladwell wrote in his book *Outliers* that "ten thousand hours is the magic number of greatness."[12] When you have practiced something for ten thousand hours, you get really good at it. What do you want your kids to get good at? Gaming and social media probably don't make the list. Yet if your children spend an average of three hours a day playing video games and using social media beginning at age nine, they will rack up the magic number of ten thousand hours by age eighteen. For context, it takes about 4,800 hours to earn a bachelor's degree.

We want our kids to become experts in life, not in gaming or social media. We have eighteen summers with our kids. Time is too precious to waste watching YouTube. Children are like wet cement and nowadays the majority of them are being imprinted by screens, not parents. But the good news is, it doesn't have to be this way.

Consider this clarifying question. *Is technology bringing your family closer together or is it driving it further apart?* Believe it or not, wherever your family is today, you can make positive changes that will impact your child for the rest of his life.

For starters, you can categorize screen time as a digital vegetable or digital candy. 'Digital vegetables' include such things as distance learning, Skyping Grandma, or listening to a podcast. "Digital candy" is pure entertainment—television sitcoms, TikTok, amusing YouTube videos. In the same way it's unhealthy to eat a lot of junk food, it's unhealthy to consume too much of this digital candy. Content does matter. Most kids don't gravitate to vegetables on their own. They're going to need your help.

And . . . this revolution often begins with making digital changes in *your* own life. The journey to using screens wisely and in a way that brings blessing to your family starts now.

Time on Devices

How many hours do your children ages 4 to 17 spend using an electronic device on a typical weekday?

77% reported 0–5 hours
12% reported 6–11 hours
11% reported 11+ hours

Average time: 4.65 hours per day[13]

Screen Media Use by Age

Under 2 — 42 minutes
2 to 4 — 2 hours and 39 minutes
5 to 8 — 2 hours and 56 minutes[14]

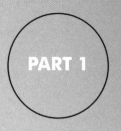

PART 1

Kids on Tech

1

Screen Time and the Brain

Digital drugs may be even more insidious and problematic than illicit drugs because we don't have our guard up about them.

—DR. NICHOLAS KARDARAS

When my (Arlene's) daughter Lucy was in fifth grade, she made a troubling comment on our way to school. "Mom, that is so sad. Look at that preschooler and her sister. They walked out of their front door holding iPads."

"Why do you think that's a problem?" I asked Lucy.

"Because they can't even walk to the car without their iPad."

Toddlers to teenagers are cradling their devices like permanent pacifiers. Screens are accessed with little effort and yield high reward. But don't be fooled. There is a cost for this cure-all entertainment system and digital soother. Many children become easily distracted. They cry easily, or become argumentative and defiant when pulled away from the screen.

For Michael, a senior in high school, video games were his life. His parents hosted a graduation party to honor Michael at their home. Michael lasted about ten minutes before he retreated to his room alone, shut the door, and began playing video games. No one could coax him out of his room, so within an hour, everyone had left the party.

Michael's brain never learned how to connect with people in social settings. But his brain had vast experience in the world of video games. According to Pew Research, 97 percent of teen boys and 83 percent of girls play games on some kind of device.[1] It turns out Michael is not alone.

Two notable takeaways have emerged from the initial data gleaned from the massive ABCD study of 11,874 children by the National Institutes of Health:

- MRI scans found significant differences in the brains of children who reported using smartphones, tablets, and video games more than seven hours a day
- Children who reported spending more than two hours a day on screens got lower scores on thinking and language tests
- The brain scans showed that kids with a lot of screen time had a premature thinning of the cortex, the outermost layer of the brain which processes information from the five senses. When your child is on screens, he is not exercising his five senses in the real world, and that part of the brain starts to decline. The cortex gets thinner over time, usually around age sixty, but that same thinning is happening much sooner now in kids.[2] This fact alone should send us scrambling to hit the pause button.

NEW DRUG ON THE BLOCK

Every year, schoolchildren participate in Red Ribbon Week to say no to drugs, and rightly so. But there is a new drug on the block that's legal, rampant, and largely accepted even for our most vulnerable. Psychiatrist and screen expert Dr. Victoria Dunckley says, "Screen time actually is very much like a drug, in fact it's like a stimulant, not unlike caffeine, or nicotine, or even cocaine. So it raises arousal levels, it changes brain chemistry."[3]

In the documentary *Screenagers,* Stanford-trained physician Dr. Delaney Ruston says, "It's amazing that there's many studies that look at MRI scans of the brain of kids who play a lot of video games, twenty hours or more of video games a week. And when they compare them to people who are addicted to, say, drugs or alcohol, their brains scans are similar. So, something is really happening on a physiological level. It's not just psychological."[4]

You might wonder how video games can be like drugs since no substance is involved. The eyes are the only outward extension of the central nervous system, affecting the brain directly. That's the gateway. "Smartphone screens light up the same area of the brain as opioids and cannabis. The rewards pathways mediated by dopamine respond to screens in a very similar way to opioids," says Anna Lembke, assistant professor of psychiatry at the Stanford University Medical Center.[5] So when you hear a parent nervously say, "It's like my son is on drugs," that's much closer to the truth than most of us realize.

Any device with an electronic screen acts like a stimulant, causing the stress hormone cortisol to rise. The more visually appealing and exciting the screen time, the more that stress hormone will rise. Cortisol prepares you to deal with an emergency; it's a "fight-or-flight" hormone. But your child isn't a caveman having to escape a predator. He is sedentary, staring at a screen, so there's this recurring mismatch between high arousal and being inert. Your child is all dressed up with nowhere to go.

When there is chronic overstimulation like this to the brain, blood flow is rerouted from the front part of the brain (the frontal lobe) to the deeper part of the brain responsible for vital functions like breathing and swallowing. This switch is significant because the frontal lobe is the most human part of our brain, regulating mood, decision-making, prioritizing, impulse control, empathy and creativity. So when your child is playing a video game and forgets to do chores or even go to the bathroom, it's because the decision-making, self-control part of his brain is turned off. It's not getting any blood. When your daughter yells at you for taking away her tablet, it's because her impulse control and empathy center have gone dark.

It's our job as parents to protect our child's brain. When that frontal lobe is given plenty of blood and physical exercise, your child will grow in self-control, mood management, and wise decision-making. Then when she is older, her brain (with that healthy frontal lobe) will be much better prepared to manage the world of screens.

Add to that the colors in the screen. Why is this important? The blue-and-white tones in a screen signal to your child's brain that it's daytime—even in the middle of the night. For millennia, blue light existed only during the daytime. Now we can see blue light 24/7, which suppresses melatonin, the hormone needed for sleep. As we have noted, school-aged children need nine to eleven hours of sleep. If your child is watching a video or playing a game before bedtime, he's going to have a harder time getting to sleep. His body clock is off. Did you know what Netflix CEO Reed Hastings said was one of his biggest competitors? *Sleep.*[6] What will you get in the morning if your child's sleep is interrupted or delayed by devices? A cranky, tired kid who isn't ready for school. Netflix, 1. Your child, 0.

Warning Signs of Too Much Screen Time

My child is irritable, tearful, depressed, or angry.
My child has a hard time focusing.
My child is forgetful and disorganized.
My child is defiant and impulsive.
My child is not empathetic and has poor social skills.

How Screen Time Impacts the Brain

Thinning cortex
Lower scores on thinking and language tests
Stress hormone cortisol rises
Blue light changes the body clock
Reduced dopamine receptors and transporters
Brain scans of video game players and drug addicts look similar
Abnormal processing (decision-making skills impaired)

A TALE OF TWO CHEMICALS

Bella, five, pushes a button on the remote control and sees a new image that makes her laugh. As Bella watches a cartoon, the neurotransmitter dopamine carries a signal of pleasure to the pleasure center of the brain. As children go for more pleasure by watching more videos or playing more games, they are pushing the dopamine level in their brain higher and higher. But as the brain's pleasure system is overused, the feeling of pleasure is diminished. The thirty minutes of video gaming that used to thrill a child now doesn't produce the same joy. So she seeks to play for longer, or to find a more stimulating game. She's looking for that fresh hit of dopamine.

Pleasure, in the right amounts, is a very good thing, but in excess, it's detrimental to your child. Just compare the difference between taking a family vacation to Disneyland to living at the theme park for a year.

Pleasure *can* be overdone. How? Here's what the scientists say. When dopamine is released from one neuron to the next, it excites that next neuron. That's what it's designed to do. But as Dr. Robert Lustig, professor emeritus of pediatrics at University of California, San Francisco says, "Neurons like to be tickled, not bludgeoned. They like to stimulate, then they like to come to rest. Chronic overstimulation of any neuron anywhere in the brain . . . will lead to neuronal cell death." Excessive dopamine kills neurons. The neurons don't "want" to die, so they have a self-defense mechanism. They downregulate the number of receptors, so it's harder for the dopamine to find a receptor with which to bind. This means the more dopamine your child produces, the more receptors go down. "Next time you need a bigger hit to get the same rush, because there are fewer receptors. And then . . . you need a bigger hit, and a bigger hit, until finally . . . the neurons actually do start to die . . . and those neurons ain't coming back. They don't regrow." says Dr. Lustig.[7]

Dopamine is wonderful in moderation, but dangerous in excess. Dopamine excites, but there's a different chemical, which inhibits: serotonin. Instead of exciting the next neuron, serotonin puts the next neuron to rest. This chemical is all about well-being, and it cannot be overdone, overused, or worn out. The brain uses serotonin to regulate mood, emotions, sleep schedule, and appetite. Serotonin is closely related to happiness, and most antidepressant drugs work by increasing serotonin levels. You can boost the level of serotonin in your child's brain by exercise and proper nutrition. But can you see how screen time fights against these two pillars of health as kids live a sedentary life, eating junk food? To increase serotonin levels in your child, aim for sixty minutes of exercise every day and a diet rich in nutrients, protein, and complex carbohydrates such as apples, carrots, and sweet potatoes. Other foods that raise serotonin levels are chicken, eggs, cheese, turkey, salmon, spinach, beans, seeds, and nuts.[8]

I'M AFRAID MY CHILD IS ADDICTED

If you've ever uttered the words "My child is addicted," you are not alone. One study asked a thousand students in ten countries to stop using technology and media for just one day. At the end of that twenty-four-hour period, many of the students repeatedly used the word "addiction." One student said, "I was itching, like a crackhead, because I could not use my phone." Others could not complete the one-day technology fast. Most said they missed their phone because it was their source of connection and comfort.[9] Many teenagers agreed with the statement "If I lose my cellphone, I lose half my brain."[10]

The *Diagnostic and Statistical Manual of Mental Health Disorders* (DSM), published by the American Psychiatric Association, recommends further research of Internet Gaming Disorder. Symptoms of Internet Gaming Disorder include:

- Gaming preoccupation
- Symptoms of withdrawal when gaming not available
- Tolerance (spending more time to achieve the same high)

- Loss of other interests
- Unsuccessful attempts to control use
- Use of gaming to lessen negative moods[11]

In China, Taiwan, and South Korea, Internet Addiction Disorder continues to climb, with as many as 30 percent of teens in these countries considered addicted.[12] In South Korea, most teenagers participate in gaming centers. Sitting in rows of small cubbies and computers, teens and young adults settle in for long periods of time to play multiplayer computer games for a small hourly fee. Teens and students in their twenties often play through the night and then go to school or work exhausted.

In extreme cases, computer addiction has turned deadly. A twenty-eight-year-old man in Korea played for fifty hours, taking just a few breaks. After he collapsed in a "PC bang" (internet café), he was rushed to the hospital where he died shortly after, presumably of heart failure because of exhaustion.[13]

Kids Who Are Addicted to Gaming . . .

Sneak around to use screens
Exhibit changes in behavior
Are only in a good mood when gaming
Increase their use over time
Freak out when forced to unplug
Choose gaming over family activities and school

Kids fall into three categories of gamers: casual, at risk, and addicted.[14] Casual players leave a game easily for another activity. At-risk gamers have more trouble, and addicts play every single day. Puzzle games such as Tetris or Solitaire are not nearly as addicting as first person shooter games. Even more addicting than the shooter games are the MMORPGs (Massively Multiplayer Online Role-Playing Game) in which a very large number of players interact with each other within a virtual game world. Be aware of the risk of addiction inherent in the games your child is choosing. Not all games are created equal.

Melanie Hempe, BSN and founder of ScreenStrong, remembers the day Adam, her freshman son in college, confessed, "Mom, I've been in bed for a week. I haven't left my dorm. *World of Warcraft* did something to me."[15] Like so many parents, Melanie Hempe had hoped her highly academic son would outgrow playing video games once he went to college. But the truth was his addiction grew exponentially worse. If a child's video game habit is a problem in high school, it will likely grow out of control in college. The struggle with an elementary school child or younger will be even worse. *Now* is the time to rescue a child from a dead-end future of gaming.

Consider a radical intervention such as an extended reset period without entertainment screens. It takes time for the hormones to shift back to normal, but as a child begins to sleep more deeply, the brain readjusts and the healing process begins. Adam did drop out of college due to excessive gaming and not finishing classes, but thankfully his story has a happy ending. He served for five years in the military (boot camp digital detox included), got back on track, and returned to complete his college career. Adam's struggle not only motivated Melanie to establish a game-free home for her younger sons but has also inspired many families to choose this option for their children. Learn more about solutions to reduce screen overuse in Melanie's book, *The Screen Strong Solution: How to Free Your Child from Addictive Screen Habits.*

THE BRAIN THROUGH THE AGES

The human brain triples in size between birth and age two, which is the largest expansion the brain will experience. Your baby comes equipped with a hundred billion neurons, and in the first three years of life, those neurons are actively building connections to each other, paving permanent roads in the brain.

When our (Arlene's) family purchased a home in new construction, there were no paved roads, only dirt roads. Today, almost twenty years later, plenty of paved roads in our area lead to supermarkets and stores, schools and houses of worship, all accessible from our house. But imagine if the dirt roads had never been paved. Talk about buyer's remorse! We would have lived on the dirt road leading to nowhere.

Your child's brain is like that new home, surrounded by dirt roads. What your child experiences in the first three years of life profoundly shapes the way he or she will think, feel, behave, and learn in adulthood. Those dirt roads are neural pathways connecting one neuron to the next. As your child sees, feels, tastes, smells, and hears, dirt roads are getting paved in her brain. But if the neurons aren't used, they are pruned and removed for efficiency.

In 1970, the average child started watching television at age four. But today the average child starts watching at four months. Screen time too early threatens this vibrant network of billions of connected neurons, the paved roads in the brain. Researchers have found the more television a child watches before age three, the more likely they are to have attention problems at age seven. For each daily hour they watch before age three, their chances of having attention problems increases by about 10 percent.[16]

Most programming for kids relies on rapid image changes to sustain attention. This preconditions a child's brain to expect high levels of stimulation, which leads to inattention later in life. There's a paved road in the brain that leads to fast-paced video games, but no road exists to prompt a child to sit still while reading a book or listening to a story. If you have a young child, it's imperative that you postpone and limit screens so your child's brain can fully develop with billions of healthy connected neurons. If your little one is more connected to an iPad than a caregiver, neurons that assist with language development or emotional stability will be pruned away from lack of use.

Perhaps you have an older child and you are afraid it is too late. It's not—your young adult's brain will continue the maturation process until age twenty-five. You still have time to positively nurture that good brain!

The second spurt of synapse formation happens in the brain just before puberty (roughly age eleven in girls, twelve in boys). Then another "pruning back" of neurons occurs in adolescence.[17]

Dr. Jay Giedd from the National Institute of Mental Health says, "Our leading hypothesis . . . is the 'use it or lose it' principle. If a teen is doing music or sports or academics, those are the cells and connections that will be hard-wired. If they're lying on the couch or playing video games or [watching] MTV, those are the cells and connections that are going [to] survive."[18] What types of brain cells and connections will be shaping your child's future?

WHAT IF MY CHILD IS LEFT BEHIND?

Dr. Gary Small, head of UCLA's memory and aging research center, conducted a very interesting experiment to demonstrate how people's brains change in response to internet use. He took a dozen experienced online users and a dozen nonusers and scanned their brains as they performed searches on Google. The computer-savvy group showed broad brain activity in the left front part of the brain associated with quick decision-making and peripheral vision, while the novices showed little if any activity in this area. The novices were then instructed to spend just one hour a day, over a five-day period, searching the internet. Following that period, the test was repeated. The new scans showed the novice group now had the same brain activity as the computer-savvy group when searching Google. In only five hours of internet use, this group had rewired their brains.[19]

Parents who are concerned their young children will be left behind if they don't board the technology plane can take comfort in this experiment. It doesn't take the brain a long time to learn how to use technology. If you had your child on the internet for five hours like the group in the experiment, no doubt they would quickly become proficient in web searches, instant messaging, video games, and photo filters.

But what about the opposite scenario? If your child grows up with screens throughout preschool and elementary school, can she take that wired brain and produce the concentration required during a classroom lecture? Can her brain readily produce empathy for a friend, or read a long passage with comprehension? These skills are much harder to pick up in a short period of time.

With increased screen use, the neural circuits that control the more traditional learning methods used for reading, writing, and sustained concentration are neglected. Nicholas Carr writes, "The world of the screen, as we're already coming to understand, is a very different place from the world of the page. A new intellectual ethic is taking hold. The pathways in our brains are once again being rerouted."[20]

Jeremy, eleven, doesn't bother to learn his vocabulary words because he knows spell-check can fix the words and texting doesn't require spelling. As Oxford neuroscientist Dr. Susan Greenfield says, "Unfortunately, the new digital world is a toxic environment for the developing minds of young people. Rather than making digital natives superlearners, it has stunted their mental growth."[21]

Traditional book readers show more activity in brain regions associated with language, memory and visual processing than in the prefrontal regions tied with decision-making and problem solving. However, internet users show extensive activity across those areas when they scan web pages. Deep reading is difficult online because the brain must evaluate links, decide where to navigate, and process distractions like advertisements. All of this pulls the brain from understanding the text at hand. Our brains online are busy making decisions and navigating through distractions, but they are not engaged in focused learning.

HOW TO STRENGTHEN YOUR CHILD'S BRAIN

Your child's brain is capable of learning math, reading, foreign languages, music, and much more. As a parent, you can build your child's brain by practicing these habits at home:

Downtime. After a good physical workout, muscles need rest to recover, right? The same is true for the brain. It's not that the brain gets tired, but it needs time in between tasks to process and consolidate the information it is learning. This free "brain time" for kids is often crowded out by screen time. Your child's brain needs to be idle from time to time. When she says, "I'm bored," that's actually good for her brain.

Physical exercise. Exercise affects your child's growing brain in many positive ways. It increases heart rate (which pumps more oxygen to the brain), reduces cortisol (the stress hormone), and burns off adrenaline. Physical activity releases brain chemicals that are natural stress fighters.

Unstructured play. Have your kids negotiate the rules and learn to play with others without any adult direction. It can be rough-and-tumble play or setting up a schoolhouse together. These activities build new circuits in the prefrontal cortex to help navigate complex social interactions.

Sleep. Certain stages of sleep are needed to cement what your child learned during the day. That learning doesn't take place if your child is sleep-deprived. The following day, if your child is sleepy, he is unable to focus and pay attention to new material. It's a vicious cycle, but thankfully it can be remedied with a few sleep strategies. Set a consistent bedtime for your child, and make his room dark, quiet, and comfortable. Don't have any screens in the bedroom. Turn off electronic devices one hour before bedtime to avoid stimulating adrenaline and preventing sleep.

Eat healthy foods. The brain uses about 20 percent of the body's calories. It needs good fuel to maintain concentration throughout the day. Serve your child nutrient-rich foods and foods with omega-3 like salmon, tuna, soybeans, and nuts. Berries, whole grains, avocados, and broccoli are other power foods for the brain.

As long as your child lives under your roof, you can make healthy adjustments starting today. Neurosurgeon Ben Carson said, "Don't let anyone turn you into a slave. You're a slave if you let the media tell you that sports and entertainment are more important than developing your brain."[22] Your child and his billion-plus brain cells are waiting to be nourished, developed, and paved—not by screens but by you as a parent.

2

Screen Time and Relationships

Your friends will determine the direction and quality of your life.
—ANDY STANLEY

Fifteen-month-old Lily sits in the shopping cart, eyes glued to her iPad. Her mom heads down the grocery store aisle with minimal interruptions. No fussing. No reaching for her mom. Her mom shops in silence. Lily never looks up into her mother's face.

Every weekday, a third grader named Henry comes home from school and grabs his device. He watches videos and plays games before and after dinner.

Aisha is a junior in high school. Last month, she sent 3,500 text messages. That's about 110 texts per day.

These scenarios have become the norm in our children's screen-driven world. It's no wonder that parents are wondering how to balance the use of technology with building relationships. Moms, dads, and grandparents are asking, "Dr. Chapman, what am I supposed to do with my children? They are on their phones or playing video games constantly. We don't have quality family time anymore. When we tell them we're going to do something as a family, they argue and head back to their screens."

Do you remember what life was like before smartphones, flat screens, and tablets? Before the digital age, children went out in their backyards and neighborhoods and played with each other. They created their own games or played endless rounds of freeze tag or hide-and-seek. Kids learned how to interact with each other. They had to deal with winning and losing, getting skinned knees, and being empathetic to a friend. Most children today are indoors for the bulk of their free time. Unfortunately, the more a child is involved in screen time, the less time there is for interaction with parents, siblings, and friends.

ANTI-SOCIAL MEDIA

What does it mean to be "social" today?

Several research studies have shown a strong correlation between social interaction and health and well-being. Yet there's not much social about kids retreating to their rooms to post selfies and comments to dozens or hundreds of followers they barely know in real life. Social media isn't very social.

Since some children in elementary school are now being introduced to social media, they are becoming more anxious about how many people "liked" the photo they just posted or how many "friends" or "followers" they have online. It's hard enough for an adult to deal with disparaging comments online—or, conversely, a lack of comments, which we interpret as "no one is interested in me." Imagine how much harder it is for children.

It's easy to say cruel things online because you don't see the effect of your words. It's one thing to post "No one likes you" and hit send from the comfort of your home. It's another thing to say the words "No one likes you" right to someone's face. We suggest you delay introducing social media to your son or daughter through adolescence. As your child grows into a teenager, she needs the firm foundation of being liked for who she is, by real people she knows. Online popularity is often based on performance, appearance, and shock value. This affection is conditional and misplaced. Your child needs to experience the unconditional love that comes from God and from you. This love can prevent problems such as resentment, feelings of being disliked, guilt, fear, and insecurity. Remember, your child is asking the question, "Do you like me?" By limiting social media, you will help her find the answer in real people who care about her instead of an online society that can be fickle and cruel.

Social Media by the Numbers

According to a Common Sense survey[1] of 13–17-year-olds in the United States:
41% had a smartphone in 2012
89% had a smartphone in 2018
34% used social media multiple times a day in 2012
70% used social media multiple times a day in 2018
54% agree that it often distracts them when they should be paying attention to the people they're with
42% agree that social media has taken away from time they could spend with friends in person

LEAVE ME ALONE, I'M GAMING

Hilarie Cash, PhD, is the cofounder of ReStart, an inpatient center in Washington State that specializes in treating screen addictions. She says, "The guys who come to us have been gaming since they were four years old. Their identities are built around their gaming prowess. As a kid, you're still a nobody, but in a game, you can make a big name for yourself. . . . You can have social status. And that's much harder and slower to achieve in the real world."[2]

Besides the risk of becoming addicted, there's also the issue of how gaming interferes with someone's life—especially how it can hurt relationships, sometimes beyond repair. Jason is a twenty-six-year-old who grew up playing video games. But when he was a teenager, he wasn't playing the massively multiplayer online games that are popular today. His brother, Danny, who's eighteen, plays for several hours a day.

"My brother used to be kind and polite when he was younger. But now, he's much different," said Jason. "After months of constant gaming, he has become rude and difficult to be around. He swears a lot more since he got his own console in his room. I think playing violent games with a bunch of strangers has a lot to do with why he acts like that."

Dr. Andrew Doan is a Johns Hopkins–educated MD with a PhD in neuroscience. He is also a recovering video game addict. He played fifty to a hundred hours a week while attending medical school on a full-ride scholarship at Hopkins. He was a "functional addict," but he was constantly sleep-deprived and chronically angry. His wife left with the kids and filed a restraining order. Today Dr. Doan has restored his relationship with his family, but only after hitting bottom and dramatically changing his ways.[3]

Although girls can become addicted to games, boys are more susceptible. Your son's future wife and your future grandchildren will profusely thank you if you raise a boy who isn't hooked on games.

I DON'T UNDERSTAND YOU

Empathy is the ability to understand and share the feelings of another. It's the missing ingredient in many friendships today. One study by the University of Michigan with data from over 14,000 students found that college students are 40 percent less empathetic than they were twenty years ago.[4]

The ease of online friendships, where you can just move on to another friend if someone is bugging you, can make real-life, messy relationships seem too frustrating. Kids are exposed to more violence in video games, which can desensitize them to pain in others, bullying, and acts of violence. The technological world consists of games, posts, and virtual worlds designed to make your child feel like the center of the universe. The environment created by screen time tends to make a child "me"-centered and not "other"-centered.

So how will your son or daughter learn how to be empathetic? The ability to understand and care for others will be gained largely through conversation, but conversation is in danger. We're texting instead of talking, heads down instead of heads up. Many moms tell me (Gary) they are talking less and less to their children and texting more. When you text, you miss facial expressions, tone and volume of voice, eye contact, and those pauses that let you know something isn't quite right. So many nuances are lost when texting.

The less we talk with our children, the less emotional connection we have with them. Texts exchange information handily, but they do not build strong emotional ties like conversation can. Today, kids aren't talking much to parents and siblings after school or in the car; they're texting. They're posting and gaming. Kids quietly swipe and choose emojis, eyes focused on a device. Think about the quality of texts between friends compared to having a real conversation. Texts aren't usually sentences or complete thoughts, ideas, or emotions. They don't tell someone's life story. They are characters like IKR (I know right), NOYB (none of your business), TTYL (talk to you later).

Our tech is advancing at lightning speed, but our conversations are deteriorating just as fast. In her book *Reclaiming Conversation: The Power of Talk in a Digital Age,* MIT professor and technology expert Sherry Turkle shares this observation from a middle school teacher: "'The [students] sit in the dining hall and look at their phones. When they share things together, what they are sharing is what is on their phones.' Is this the new conversation? If so, it is not doing the work of the old conversation. As these teachers see it, the old conversation taught empathy. These students seem to understand each other less."[5]

Josh Burnette, coauthor of *Adulting 101* and restaurant owner, is also concerned about this "new conversation." He observes, "I'll walk by a table of my team members all sitting down on break together, which is wonderful, but all four of them will be on their phones, heads down, not engaging with each other. I think it's preventing them from having social skills such as quick responses to dialogue. Everything is filtered through the phone."[6]

Researchers have found that the mere presence of a phone makes you feel less close and connected to your friends. Experimenting with conversations with and without a phone, researchers discovered when the phone was absent, something else became present: closeness, trust, and perceptions of empathy. But when the phone was on the table within reach, a person's attention was divided, inhibiting any kind of meaningful conversation.[7]

Let's make a practice of leaving our phones out of sight when talking with our kids at mealtimes, car rides, and bedtime. Talk with your child in places like the doctor's office and the grocery store. These are perfect places to practice people skills with your kids. Put your phone in your pocket and teach your child how to notice the cashier's name and use it. Teach her to ask, "So how is your day going, Wendy?" It's something so simple, but it gets your child used to making conversation with others. It puts the focus on someone else and plants the seed of empathy in your child's heart.

I (Arlene) was at the dentist with my girls for their regular cleaning. I smiled as I heard my ten-year-old ask our longtime dentist, "How's your week going?" and they had a brief conversation before she "opened wide" for her cleaning. Kids need to feel comfortable making conversation with adults and other kids, becoming more competent with every opportunity. These conversations will make it much easier to empathize with others in the future, making your son or daughter the kind of friend someone wants for life. (And never underestimate the impact of being engaging and socially adept in the business world.)

BUT MY CHILD IS SHY

Seated next to other parents, Nikki pulled out a magazine from her purse to read while waiting for her daughter to finish ballet practice. Before reading, she decided to introduce herself to the mom next to her. "Hi, I'm Nikki. What's your name?"

"Oh, nice to meet you," said the other lady, who was sitting next to a boy who looked about eight. "I'm Grace, and this is my son Peter." She gestured toward Peter and turned towards him. "Peter, say hi to Miss Nikki."

Peter continued to look down at his video game. His mother's words didn't faze him. After pausing a moment, his mom said sheepishly, "Sorry about that. Peter is very shy. He's always been that way."

Although Peter was adept at making friends at school, his mother had never forced him to engage with others because she thought Peter was "shy" and would eventually come around on his own. Kids like Peter can easily hide behind electronic screens to avoid interactions with others that seem unpleasant or unnecessary. And studies show increasing numbers of young people who report being shy. Many experts believe this rising number is partially due to the social isolation that comes with being digitally connected. But most kids can be taught to interact with others with relative ease, if we can just get them to put down their screens.

When referring to shyness, we are talking about a child who is nervous and uncomfortable meeting and talking to people. Shy children don't adapt as well as their peers in the classroom or playground because they are timid in the company of others. The longer a child practices the pattern of avoiding new people and withdrawing from social settings, the more of a hindrance this will be in adult life.

However, do not confuse being shy with being quiet. If one of your children is the life of the party, but the other one hardly says a word in public, it doesn't mean that your quieter child is shy. Outgoing, extroverted, talkative children are the objects of much praise. But quieter, introverted children bring strengths such as being great listeners and analytic thinkers.

If you are wondering what is healthy and what is unhealthy when it comes to a child who is quiet and reserved, consider these characteristics:

Healthy	Unhealthy
Makes eye contact with others	Avoids eye contact with others
Polite	Rude, unresponsive
Content	Dissatisfied
Generally exhibits good behavior	Has behavioral problems
People are comfortable with him	People are not comfortable with him

Don't think of your child as shy just because he is quiet. Maybe he won't raise his hand in class, but he'll eagerly discuss a subject in a small group. It's okay if your child is more reserved than others. And even if your child is afraid of new people and new situations, avoid labeling him as shy. When a child hears over and over that he is shy, it gives him an excuse for not developing social skills. A child can say, "Oh, I'm just shy," giving him a pass to skip politeness and conversation. For some children, being shy becomes very convenient. Boys and girls who have trouble with shyness may retreat too much to the screen for electronic companionship. Introverted and extroverted children have this in common: they all have to learn what's appropriate when interacting with people. It's okay to nudge your child to practice common courtesies such as shaking someone's hand or saying "Nice to meet you."

SCREEN TIME RECOMMENDATIONS FOR HEALTHY RELATIONSHIPS

All screen media are not equal, which makes it impractical to come up with a one-size-fits-all time limit recommendation for the healthy, relational family. Playing Scrabble with Grandma online is different than playing a first-person shooter game. *Creating* videos is different than *consuming* videos. Watching a show with your parent and discussing it is different than watching unsupervised. The American Academy of Pediatrics (AAP) offers an online media time calculator you can use to take a snapshot of your family's current screen habits. You can also create a personalized family media plan at healthychildren.org.

Here are a few of the AAP recommendations:[8]

- For children younger than eighteen months, avoid screen media.
- For children eighteen months to two years, choose high-quality programming and watch it with your children.
- For children two to five years, limit screen use to one hour per day of high-quality programs. Parents should view content together to help them understand what they are seeing.
- For children six and older, place consistent limits on the time spent using media and the types of media.
- Make sure media does not take the place of adequate sleep, physical activity, and other behaviors necessary for health.
- Designate media-free time, such as dinner or driving, as well as media-free locations such as bedrooms.

The temptation to use screens to entertain babies and toddlers is stronger than ever. You almost feel obligated as a parent to utilize the latest and greatest educational software available. But the AAP reports adverse health effects of direct media use as well as parental media use (background media) in the life of a young child. Children under two years of age process information differently than older children because they are at an earlier stage of cognitive development. You may be surprised to learn that two studies have found that watching a program like *Sesame Street* has a negative effect on language development for children younger than two.[9] While you may think a television show or phone app is doing a great job teaching your baby the ABCs, media use has not been proven to promote language skills in this age group. Young children learn language best when it's presented by a live person, not on a screen.

A study from 2017 reported that nearly half (49%) of children age eight or under often or sometimes watch TV or videos or play video games in the hour before bedtime. Video viewing is the predominant screen activity for children eight or under, and 42 percent say TV is on at home "always" or "most of the time," regardless of whether someone is watching it.[10]

What is the effect of this background media on a child? Studies have shown that when the television is on, it may be background noise to the child, but it often moves to the foreground for the parent. A child's ability to learn language is directly related to the amount of talk time he or she has with a parent. When the television is on, Mom or Dad is less likely to engage in conversation, resulting in a smaller vocabulary for that child.

Researchers examined toddlers aged one, two, and three and found that background television not only reduced the length of time that a child played, but it also reduced the child's focused attention during play.[11] Other studies suggest that background media might interfere with cognitive processing, memory, and reading comprehension. In spite of these negative effects, almost one-third of children have a television in their bedroom by age three.[12] We do not believe it is wise for any child, regardless of age, to have a television in their own room. Many of these young children are using the TV as a sleep aid. However, television viewing before falling asleep is associated with irregular sleep schedules and poor sleep habits that affect mood, behavior, learning, and relationships.

Parents, we must think about the purpose of technology in our homes, and then design a media plan that supports those goals. Once you have a plan, stick with it. Your kids probably won't say, "Mom, it's so great we're cutting back to just half hour of YouTube a day. That's going to give me so much more time to get my reading done!" No, your child is going to kick and scream and exert tremendous pressure so you'll cave in. Imagine yourself as a redwood tree, tall, immovable, with roots underneath the surface. No matter what your child says, you will not be moved.

"Parents are in a more powerful position than they realize."

Dr. Douglas Gentile from Iowa State University studied more than 1,400 families in two states. His team found that parents who set limits on the amount and content of children's media make a significant difference in terms of kids getting more sleep, doing better in school, being more pro-social, being less aggressive, and being at lower risk for obesity. He said, "Parents are in a more powerful position than they realize."[13] Friend, you have more power than you think to help your child have healthy relationships based on empathy and love, not screens.

3

Screen Time and Safety

The Fear-of-God builds up confidence,
and makes a world safe for your children.
—PROVERBS 14:26, *THE MESSAGE*

Amy and Bill tried their best to create a safe online environment for their ten-year-old daughter, Kendra. Screen time was limited to two hours per day, and no electronic devices were allowed in her bedroom. Kendra used the computer or phone in a common area like the kitchen table or family room. With internet filters installed on the computer and phones, Kendra's parents felt secure about her screen time.

What they didn't realize was Kendra's growing affection for a popular social networking site for kids. She logged in every day to play games, chat with screen friends, and read the fashion blog. Although the website was marketed as safe for kids, she was watching trailers for PG-13 movies and in the chat room reading responses to "How do I know if he likes me?" Kendra became more self-conscious about her appearance and started worrying because no boys at school seemed to like her. She was being influenced by the comments she read online from other kids, and her parents didn't know anything about it. Just because something says it's "safe for kids" doesn't mean it is.

RECOMMENDED VIDEOS, REALLY?

I (Arlene) was watching a Pixar short "For the Birds" with my then-ten-year-old daughter, Lucy, on YouTube. Lucy's teacher had recommended the animated short film to illustrate the concept of cause and effect. The video was funny and totally safe for my daughter to watch. But do you know what cued up next? One video featuring drag queens and another one titled "Dead by Daylight." I could not believe it. Much more than the television of yesteryear, YouTube plays a prominent role in directing what our children are seeing and watching by cueing up what video plays next. YouTube's algorithm isn't exactly family-friendly—quite the opposite.

Daily online video watching is going through the roof, doubling in four years from 24 percent to 56 percent among eight- to twelve-year-olds.[1] According to a Pew Research study, 81 percent of all parents with children age eleven or younger say they let their child watch videos on YouTube. (YouTube states that its platform is not appropriate for children younger than thirteen.) About two-thirds of users (64%) say they sometimes encounter videos that seem obviously false, while 60 percent report encountering videos that show people engaging in dangerous or troubling behavior. When parents of young children were surveyed, 61 percent report encountering content unsuitable for children like my drag queen and "Dead by Daylight" video experiences.[2]

YouTube Kids offers more kid-friendly fare, but even that is not foolproof. For example, unnamed YouTube creators manipulated content from well-known children's franchises such as Peppa Pig, PAW Patrol, and Mickey Mouse. These videos appeared innocuous in the first few minutes but became progressively darker with time. CNBC reported on an image of a Bubble Guppies character pole-dancing in a bar. Doctors and "mental health experts warn that YouTube is a growing source of anxiety and inappropriate sexual behavior among kids" under thirteen.[3]

YouTube says it's trying to remedy these problems, but with four hundred hours of video uploaded to YouTube every *minute*, blocking all harmful content is impossible. We as parents must do something to make sure our kids are not harmed by what they see on YouTube. In her book *Strong Fathers, Strong Daughters*, Dr. Meg Meeker wrote about a little girl who suddenly became fearful of her father. Turns out the girl had watched a man who was abusive to a woman on television. She was presented with this image and as a child, she didn't know how to distinguish reality from non-reality. She pulled back from her father and began not to trust him simply because of what she saw on TV![4] We must make a commitment to be actively involved with what our kids are watching. Once you find those parent-approved programs, YouTube videos, and personalities, subscribe to those channels so your child doesn't have to hunt around looking for something to watch.

Internet Hall of Shame Statistics

22% of teen girls say they posted nude or semi-nude photos or videos of themselves online.

70% of children 7–18 years old have accidentally encountered online porn, often through a web search while doing homework.

65% of 8–14-year-olds have been involved in a cyberbullying incident.

The FBI reports a 2,000% increase in the number of child pornography images on the internet since 1996.[5]

THE POISON OF PORN

The days of going to a seedy part of town to browse an adult bookstore are long over. Porn is available on devices that we use every day—phones, computers, and tablets. A child could simply be curious because they heard someone at school talk about sex or kissing. Or they may accidentally click on a link while doing a Google search. Although viewing porn once probably won't have long-term effects on your child, viewing it on a regular basis will. The more graphic the porn, the more destructive to the mind and heart of your child.

When you view the body of a person and find that stimulating, it's extremely difficult to get those pictures out of your mind. Your child will likely carry those pictures into future dating relationships and marriage. Pornography misinforms children and confuses them about human sexuality. There is the devaluing of women, the exaltation of "perfect" body types, and false expectations that will be carried into a future relationship. Kids view porn secretly, which is dishonoring to their parents while causing shame in the heart of the child. You may think your child or tween is too young to talk about sex, but they are getting messages about sex in school, social media, YouTube, movies, and music. If you don't say a word about sex until you catch your child looking at porn, he or she is going to think, "What's going on here? You've never even talked to me about this before!"

So start early and explain to your child that there are males and females in the world. Using appropriate drawings, show what a male body looks like and what a female body looks like. Ask the question, "Why do we wear clothes?" All human cultures make coverings because some parts of the body are meant to be private. Have an honest and open talk about what is going to happen to your child's body when he or she becomes a teenager. Explaining these things long before they happen helps your child understand that sexuality is not a taboo topic.

You can talk to your child about Adam and Eve and how God clothed them for a reason. Then you can talk about pornography and how porn violates that decency. Explain that someday, pictures of naked people or partially naked people may pop up on the screen. When that happens, instruct your child to close that window right away and to come and tell you about it.

We suggest having several short conversations about sexuality and porn, so it's not just one long marathon talk where your child is wondering, "When will this be over?" Remember to bring this topic up more frequently as your children become tweens. Your children need and want your guidance to understand how their bodies work and how to navigate their sexual feelings. Preteens are now sending or posting nude pictures of themselves because they've been dared to, or because they want attention. A study from *JAMA Pediatrics* of eleven- to seventeen-year-olds found that 14.8 percent sent sexts and 27.4 percent received them.[6]

Let your children know there will be consequences if you find out they are viewing or creating pornography. Enforce boundaries while keeping your tone calm and your heart soft toward your child. Admitting to pornography is embarrassing, and if a child feels that his parent will shame him, he may work very hard to keep his pornography use a secret.

If you discover your child is viewing pornography regularly and cannot seem to stop, we recommend you seek a professional counselor who can direct your child away from this unhealthy behavior. Do not allow your son or daughter to be brought up with pornography. Its negative effects could impact your child into adulthood. My (Arlene's) son, who is a high school junior, doesn't have a phone. I believe it's safer for Ethan to bike home from school without a phone than to have easy access to porn through a phone in his pocket.

Closely related to pornography is human trafficking, which is the fastest-growing organized crime activity in the United States. The International Labour Organization estimates that there are 40 million victims of human trafficking globally, and 25 percent of them are children.[7] Chat rooms for kids are not only problematic because of cyberbullying, but they are also a nesting place for predators. Explain to your child that people in chat rooms may not be who they seem to be. A thirty-seven-year-old mom posed as an eleven-year-old girl named Bailey, in partnership with Bark, an organization that uses AI (artificial intelligence) to alert parents and schools when children are experiencing cyberbullying, threats of violence, and targeting by sexual predators. This mom posted a photo on Instagram of herself smiling (in disguise with the help of clothing, background, hairstyling, and photo manipulation) with the caption: *v excitedd to see my friends this weekend at carly's party! Ilysm!!* By the end of two-and-a-half hours after posting, "Bailey" received seven video calls, ignored another two dozen of them, text-chatted with seventeen men (some who had messaged repeatedly), and seen the genitalia of eleven of these. By the end of one week, over fifty-two men reached out to an eleven-year-old girl. The script seen was largely the same:

You're so pretty.

You should be a model.

I'm older than you.

What would you do if you were here baby?

And then the messages get sexual.[8] Our daughters need to be educated about—and protected from—these dangers. Young people who successfully avoid being victimized online are very savvy about the safety issues of the Internet, and they value their privacy.

THE APPS ARE WATCHING

Websites and mobile apps collect significant amounts of personal information from children. When kids are asked to register with a site in order to play a game or enter a contest, they may be asked to input their name, street address or city, birthday, or favorite activities. This information can be used to create customer lists, which are sold to businesses. Tell your child never to share his or her birthday, address, or credit card number online without consulting you first.

Teach your kids that the apps are watching. *Wall Street Journal* columnist Joanna Stern tested eighty apps and found they were sharing reams of her personal data. Kids' apps had an average of three third-party trackers per app. A Curious George app called "Curious World," aimed toward children ages two to seven, was sending kids' names and ages to Facebook. Seven of those "trackers" were discovered on Curious World. Innocent-looking apps are sending your child's data to help advertisers, and to gather analytics to make the apps even more engaging for users.[9]

Social networking sites require that a child be at least thirteen to sign up. That's because the Children's Online Privacy Protection Act (COPPA) restricts websites from collecting personal data about minors. However, as you may know from your own experience or from friends, many children lie about their age, with some 7.5 million minors allegedly signing on.[10] If your eleven-year-old wants to be on social media with her classmates and her grandma, what's the harm? For starters, there is the wasted time online that could be used for much healthier activities. Then there is the matter of strangers seeing your child's profile. Think of how easy it is for a predator who is disguised online as a twelve-year-old to know a lot about your child through social media. He can look at photos and figure out what school your child attends, what her interests are, and what her patterns are, like stopping at Starbucks for a frappucino every Friday. He can befriend her online, pretending to be a cute teenage boy, and know exactly what she likes to talk about. We must warn our kids to be suspicious about anyone they do not know in real life.

Privacy must be vigilantly guarded by parents in this digital age. Many children and tweens do not yet possess the wisdom to understand the value of privacy. Instruct your kids not to share their passwords with anyone, even best friends. Disable location services on every app except ones like Google maps when using it, so a stranger cannot easily see where your child is located. Kids live in the moment. They are not thinking, "Hmm . . . posting this photo and comment may really hurt me in the future." Something meant for one friend can be screenshotted and shared with the world. A text or social media comment can be taken out of context. We need to coach our kids that their posts are public, not private. Private conversations need to happen offline, face-to-face, not on the superhighway of the online world for all to see.

SAFE FROM HEAD TO TOE

A woman approached me (Arlene) after a speaking engagement about technology. She had struggled with rashes on her wrist and lower arm for months, purchasing expensive creams and consulting dermatologists. Finally, she tried an experiment to cut back on her phone use—and the rashes cleared up. She was shocked to discover her constant exposure to the phone was causing the rashes. Although her affliction may be uncommon, it illustrates the connection between increased technology use and physical health. All computers emit EMFs (electromagnetic field exposures) on many different frequencies. When your child's laptop or tablet is wirelessly connected to the internet, they are being exposed to radiation.

It's widely accepted that this radiation level is very low. But since kids are being exposed to this radiation younger and younger, and for longer and longer periods of time, it merits a second look.

The US Food and Drug Administration nominated cellphones for study by the National Toxicology Program (NTP) because of widespread public use of cellphones and limited knowledge about potential health risks from long-term exposure. After ten years of study and 30 million dollars, the NTP concluded there is clear evidence that male rats exposed to high levels of radio-frequency radiation, like that used in 2G and 3G cellphones, developed cancerous heart tumors.[11]

The rat's entire body was exposed to radiation. In humans, that radiation is localized to the specific tissues close to where they are holding the phone (or their laps where their tablets are resting). Because laptops and tablets are used in such close proximity to the body, they are particularly dangerous, especially for kids. An easy habit to introduce to your child is setting the tablet on a table to watch videos, instead of a lap. Not only will this lessen the impact of radiation, it makes it less comfortable to watch videos 24/7.

Radiation is not the only physical concern. Myopia (nearsightedness) is dramatically on the rise. In East Asia, 80 to 90 percent of young adults have myopia.[12] Why the dramatic uptick? We are spending too much time focusing on screens a few inches away and too little time looking into the distance. We are inside, not outside. One way to alleviate eyestrain is to follow the 20-20-20 rule: every 20 minutes, stare at an object 20 feet away for 20 seconds.

Let's move from the eyes to the ears. Listening to music for just fifteen minutes at 100 decibels can damage hearing. My husband, James, often tells our kids emphatically, "You never get that hearing back!" As a reference, normal conversation is about 60dB, a lawnmower is 90 dB, and a loud rock concert is about 120 dB. If you can't hear anything going on around you when listening on earbuds, the sound level is too high. Lifelong hearing loss is increasing among teens at alarming rates, with the World Health Organization estimating 1.1 billion young people at risk. One in five teenagers have some form of hearing loss, a rate about 30 percent higher than in the 1980s and '90s.[13] When using headphones, you can apply the 60/60 rule: keep the volume under 60 percent and only listen for a maximum of 60 minutes a day.[14]

"Text neck" is becoming commonplace as phone users spend an average of two to four hours per day hunched over devices.[15] Doctors compare the effects to bending a finger all the way back and holding it there for about an hour. Ouch! There's also "smartphone thumbs," which is basically tendinitis caused by overuse from gaming and texting. Your child probably isn't complaining of physical pain yet, but they probably will in their twenties and thirties if their habits continue.

Perhaps the most dangerous side effect of screen media exposure is obesity, one of the most challenging public health problems facing developed and developing countries around the world. More than 2 billion adults and children around the world are overweight or obese, suffering health problems due to weight.[16] Screen media use is one of the best-documented causes of obesity in children. Randomized controlled trials of reducing screen time in communities have reduced weight gain in children, demonstrating a cause-and-effect relationship. Evidence suggests that is because children eat more when they are viewing, and they are exposed to high-calorie, low-nutrient foods and beverages which are heavily marketed. That influences what they ask for, what they buy, and what they eat. Screen time often robs a child of a good night's sleep, which also contributes to overeating and poor health.[17]

When we think of screen time safety, we often think of internet filters, monitoring apps, and keeping predators far away from our kids. But perhaps a greater (and far more common) danger is the early deterioration of our child's health, and the lifelong physical limitations and diseases that will follow.

BUT EVERYONE ELSE HAS A PHONE!

Many fifth and sixth graders at my kids' school have a phone just like mine. It's unfortunate to see many kids looking down at phones after school instead of talking to their friends. You probably know children that young or younger who have their own phones. So how young is too young for a smartphone? Every child and family circumstance is different, so there's no one answer. Ask the questions, "What does my child need a phone for?" and "Is my child ready to handle a phone?" Weigh the benefits against the drawbacks. Children in elementary school do not need access to the internet on their phones. Giving a child the responsibility of browsing the internet safely is an unreasonable expectation. It's like letting a child loose alone in a mall which has adult bookstores, child predators, and drug dealers, and hoping he or she will stay out of trouble.

If you are going to give a child a phone (and we suggest waiting for eighth grade or high school), start with a basic phone with no internet access and see how your child handles it. For the first month, you might consider having your child use the phone only to text or call parents and closest friends. Provide freedom gradually, much like starting with training wheels on a bicycle (dumb phone) and then taking those training wheels off when your child has demonstrated readiness (smartphone). You can create a phone contract from the start so expectations of use are clearly communicated and there are no surprises. Your contract may include the following:

> I will not give my phone number to anyone unless I clear it with my parents.
>
> I will not bring my phone into the classroom if it is prohibited.
>
> I will answer calls from my parents unless I am in class.
>
> I will pay for any charges above and beyond the usual monthly fee.

But do keep in mind that contracts are typically between adults; most children are not mature enough to abide by a contract alone. Kids need clear boundaries and consequences when rules are broken.

Screen-Safe Family Pledge

You can use the following pledge as a starting point for your child and modify it to fit your family's needs.

I will never give out personal information such as my last name, address, or phone number.

I will not give out the name of my school, city, or parent's workplace.

I will not share my passwords with anyone.

I will follow the time limits that my family sets.

I will allow my parents to check into my media history whenever they think it is necessary.

I will only have online interactions with people I know in real life.

I will tell my mom or dad right away if anything I see makes me uncomfortable or if anyone asks to meet me.

I will not stay on or click on a page that says, "For Over 18 Years Only."

I will not download any pictures or files unless a parent has approved it.

I will not send pictures of myself or my family to anyone online without my parent's permission.

I will not say anything online that I wouldn't say in real life.

HOME SAFE HOME

Your home should be a place of security for your child, a warm and loving environment. When that's the case, your child usually won't go looking for belonging and connection in an unsafe online world. Home isn't meant to be a place where individual family members retreat to their screens to become engrossed in the news of politics or the playground. In today's digital world, you must think about the role screens will play in your home. Perhaps it's unrealistic to have a screen-free home, but what about a screen-smart and screen-safe home?

Perhaps it's unrealistic to have a screen-free home, but what about a screen-smart and screen-safe home?

One good rule of thumb is to keep all electronic media out of the children's rooms, whether your child is a toddler or teen. You don't know what goes on after the door is closed and the lights go out. Watching screens before bedtime in a child's room can interrupt healthy sleep patterns, not to mention give a child unsupervised access to all sorts of objectionable content.

The family computer or tablet should be used in an open location that everyone can see. Many families collect all electronic devices at night, placing cellphones, tablets, and gaming devices in a bin that's stored in the parents' bedroom overnight. If you've allowed screens in your child's room, you can start with an apology that might sound like this: "I've allowed you to have a screen in your room, but I realize that's not the best for your health. I'm sorry and I am going to make a change." Your child most likely isn't going to nominate you for "Parent of the Year" in that moment, so brace for some opposition and stand firm.

Besides keeping tabs on *where* the electronics are in your

home, you can practice internet safety by filtering *what* can be viewed. The ability to pause the internet, lock individual devices, and block and filter content is usually available with the parental control features already built into your device's operating system. You can check publications such as *PC Magazine* for reviews of the most current parental control software. Using filters on your computers and phones is a recommended practice, but of course, it does not guarantee that your child will not see something inappropriate. Some kids will stumble upon something too sexual or violent; other kids will seek it out. A child who is determined to view something that has been declared off-limits can find a way around filters and monitoring systems. Don't fall into a false sense of security simply because you have a first-rate internet safety system in place.

Around the dinner table, I (Arlene) asked my children what they thought about parents monitoring every text, social media post, and online interaction of their kids. There is a tension between over-monitoring and under-monitoring. Noelle, who was in eighth grade at the time, suggested, "Parents shouldn't give their children phones and social media until they think they are ready to handle it well on their own."

My children, who are currently in sixth, ninth, and eleventh grade, do not have smartphones or social media accounts. That's a safety and health decision we've intentionally made so that when they do start, they'll be better equipped to handle it well—on their own. We can't monitor every click, swipe, and view in our child's life. We might not catch every predator or toxic person from reaching out to our kids. Eventually, the best filter for a growing child is his or her own eyes and ears, as parents teach what is healthy and unhealthy in real life and on screens.

4

Screen Time and Emotional Health

As a psychologist, I can tell you that there are people who look very good in a group, but they're very different in a one-on-one situation.
—DR. HENRY CLOUD

Six-year-old Ruby came home in tears again. Since transferring to a new school, she hadn't been able to make friends after three weeks. Today at lunch she had made a brave attempt to sit next to some girls from class, but they looked up and said, "Sorry, we don't have any more space at this table." She quietly found another place to sit in the cafeteria as she fought back tears.

Since Ruby wasn't having much success in the friend department, she stopped trying to initiate conversations at recess. She became more withdrawn in the classroom, often avoiding eye contact with her classmates and teacher. At home, she started watching a lot more YouTube after school.

Eric, eleven, loved playing soccer but dreaded going to practice. One of his teammates, Luke, twelve, constantly made fun of him. He'd say things like, "If you want to score, don't pass the ball to Eric," and "Who taught you to play? A bunch of girls?" Eric didn't tell his parents about the bullying. Instead he threw himself into his video games—where he was the one calling the shots.

When kids like Ruby and Eric have trouble in social settings, it's easier than ever to retreat to the safety of screens. If you feel left out, just fiddle with a smartphone or play a video game. You'll look busy, occupied, and important. Being with screens is a lot easier than being with people. Your tablet doesn't care if you're having a bad hair day. You can simply be with a game or video that makes you feel connected to something with very little effort. But screen time in the wrong amounts or of the wrong content can cause further damage to your child's emotional health.

24/7 BULLYING

Decades ago, when I (Arlene) was in elementary school, there weren't many Asians in my class. A boy named John would sometimes chase me around the playground, taunting "China Girl, China Girl." I'd run into the bathroom and wait until recess was over to come out. That situation was just between my childhood recess bully and me.

Imagine if kids back then had been "weaponized" with smartphones. He'd post "China Girl, China Girl" and my playground drama would spread. When I walked into class the next day, it wouldn't just be John making fun of me, it would be Mike, Zoe, Samuel, and Brittany. Bullies used to just have a few minutes before or after school to make fun of their targets, or as in my case, recess. Now they can do it 24/7. Damaging photographs and cruel comments live on, not limited to a geographic location anymore. There are parents who have removed their daughters from schools because of bullying on social media, only to have the bullies follow her to the new school from the convenience of their living rooms, using their phones.

Cyberbullying is deliberately using digital media to repeatedly threaten, harass, mistreat, or make fun of another person. Social media has provided a free and easily accessed platform for bullies to continue their threats and taunts long after school is out. Every embarrassing moment, every piece of gossip, every mistake has the potential to be recorded, shared, and commented upon. The screen allows an anonymity that can cushion the user from suffering any consequences. It's easier than ever to hurt another person—just hit the send button.

It's easier than ever to hurt another person—just hit the send button.

According to one national survey of 4,500 twelve- to seventeen-year-olds:[1]

34 percent have experienced cyberbullying.

17 percent have experienced cyberbullying in the last 30 days.

4 out of 5 of those cyberbullied said mean comments were posted.

70 percent of those cyberbullied said someone spread rumors about them.

64 percent of those cyberbullied said it really affected their ability to learn and feel safe at school.

12 percent admit they had cyberbullied others. The most common behaviors were spreading rumors (60%), posting mean comments (58%), and threatening to hurt someone (54%).

Kids making fun of one another and saying hateful words is

nothing new. But technology can magnify and spread a hurtful comment to damage and frighten a child like never before. Young children are not emotionally equipped to handle digital hits to their self-esteem. Kids are posting each other's secrets, stealing passwords, and attacking others while posing as someone else, and taking inappropriate pictures to share online to embarrass.

As parents, we are responsible to foster the mental and emotional health of our children. We cannot throw up our hands and say, "I just don't understand the latest technology." Here are a few warning signs a child is being cyberbullied:[2]

- Noticeable increases or decreases in device use, including texting.
- Exhibiting emotional responses (laughter, anger, upset) to what they are seeing on their device.
- Hiding their device when others are near and avoiding discussion about what they are doing on the device.
- Social media accounts are shut down or new ones appear.
- Avoiding social situations that were enjoyed in the past.
- Becoming withdrawn or depressed, losing interest in people and activities.

A child lacking essential relational skills might become a controlling bully who lacks empathy and treats others cruelty. Or she may become a victim of bullying who doesn't know how to ask for help. You can help your child develop a bully-proof heart by sharing these guidelines:

- Tell them to report any bullying incidents to you.
- Block bullies and don't ever respond to their comments.
- Talk about the dangers of attacking others online.
- Teach your child to never post anything she wouldn't be comfortable showing you or her teacher.

- If your child receives a hurtful comment, tell him five things you like about him.

If your child is the one who is doing the bullying, let him know you are not going to condemn him. He may feel guilty about what he has done and never express his feelings again, especially if he is responsive to authority. Part of training is to let him know that you accept him as a person and always want to know how he is feeling, whether happy, sad, or angry. From that place of love, you can work with him to correct his behavior in the future. One consequence may be to take the phone or iPad away for two days for the first offense. If it happens again, you can restrict their electronic use for a longer period of time.

THE FAST AND ANXIOUS TRACK OF TECHNOLOGY

Bree, a likeable eleven-year-old, picks up her phone first thing in the morning. What should she post? How does she want to portray herself to others? Is she getting enough likes? It's time to build her brand.[3] To build and maintain a personal brand is an exhausting job, and yet that is what kids are doing on social media. No wonder so many kids are struggling with anxiety and depression, obsessing about their appearance and worrying about where they fit in.

A group of psychiatrists at Johns Hopkins studied the rising rate of depression among teens. The odds of adolescents suffering from clinical depression grew by 37 percent from 2005 to 2014.[4] For the study, a depressive state was defined as when symptoms (such as loss of interest or pleasure in daily activities) persist for two weeks or more. The research dates correlate with the early days of the iPhone and Facebook. Coincidence? We don't think so. Being on your phone or tablet leads to less face-to-face time and meaningful conversation—two things that are essential to emotional health.

Anxiety is also on the rise. Since 1985, the Higher Education Research Institute at UCLA has been asking incoming freshmen if they "felt overwhelmed" by all they had to do. In 1985, 18 percent replied yes. By 2000, the number climbed to 28 percent, and by 2016, to almost 41 percent. This same pattern appears when comparing modern-day teens to teens in their grandparents' or great-grandparents' era. When psychologist Jean Twenge looked at survey results from more than 77,500 high school and college students over the decades, she found anxiety and depression were six times more common today than in 1938. Yet our way of life is so much easier. Grocery stores are fully stocked and technology brings speedy answers to just about any question. But we are more susceptible to anxiety and depression than our great-grandparents. We've traded in simpler times for the fast and anxious track of technology.[5]

A study by researchers at the University of California, Berkeley, found that nearly half of Americans report feeling alone. One of the causes: sleep deprivation. "Sleep deprivation can turn us into social lepers," said UC Berkeley professor Matthew Walker. This "cycle may be a significant contributing factor to the public-health crisis that is loneliness." The past decade has seen a steep climb in both loneliness and lack of sleep. Members of Generation Z (adults age eighteen to twenty-two for the study) say they are the loneliest generation and claim to be in worse health than older generations. The child or teen who's gaming or streaming videos way past bedtime isn't only losing precious sleep, he or she is opening the door for many other problems emotionally, mentally, and spiritually.[6]

Jean Twenge's research also reveals that the more time teen girls spend on social media and smartphones, the more likely they are to be depressed and exhibit suicide-related behaviors. "Boys' depressive symptoms increased by 21 percent from 2012 to 2015, while girls' increased by 50 percent."[7] Another study in the journal *Cyberpsychology, Behavior and Social Networking* suggested middle- and high-schoolers who are heavy users of social media (spending more than two hours a day) are more likely to report poor mental health and psychological distress.[8]

We've always been influenced by what our friends said about us, but with social media it's so much easier to say negative things or to see that other people are having fun with friends and we aren't. We can talk with our kids and ask questions like, "How did people respond to your post? How did that make you feel?" It's important to engage in conversation so your child doesn't internalize too deeply what they are reading, making too much of their friend's lack of response or negative comments. Lovingly remind your child that our value is not in what other people say or don't say. Children (and adults) can have feelings like "I'm not good enough" or "No one likes me." If the home life is negative and kids are hearing things like "You're not very good in math" from Mom or Dad, that is going to contribute to poor emotional health. Many of us adults are living with our own emotional struggles, but for the sake of our kids, we must learn how to create a healthy emotional environment at home.

Tuning into emotional or behavioral cues is important in identifying potential problems and working with your son or daughter. If you see your child withdrawing or hear them saying or writing negative things about themselves, it's extremely important that you open up conversation about that. The sooner you act, the better. Don't ignore it, and if the negative statements persist, we recommend you find a good counselor to work with your child.

Signs of Emotional Stress

Your child is more prone to mood swings.
Your child withdraws from activities.
Your child routinely expresses worries.
Your child is complaining, crying, or displaying fearful reactions.
Your child is clinging to a parent or teacher.
Your child is sleeping too much or too little.
Your child is eating too much or too little.[9]

BREAKING THE CHAINS OF HOPELESSNESS

Saddleback Church pastor and bestselling author Rick Warren and his wife, Kay, have experienced one of life's greatest tragedies—the suicide of their twenty-seven-year-old son, Matthew. Matthew was diagnosed with clinical depression at age seven, and later with ADHD and panic attacks. He began having suicidal thoughts at age twelve. Kay Warren said, "I lived for years with the fear and the dread that he'd take his life. That he actually took his life was my worst nightmare come true." Out of their pain and passion to help others, the Warrens have pushed mental health to the forefront of Saddleback Church's ministries.

The first time Rick Warren prayed publicly in church for people living with mental illness, the response from the congregation was palpable. Following the services, dozens of men and women who were living with mental illness or had a loved one with mental illness lined up to hug him and thank him for bringing their struggle into the light. They said things like, "I've kept my illness a secret at church. I didn't know it was okay to talk about it."

That simple prayer changed the atmosphere at the church, making it safer to talk openly about depression, anxiety, bipolar disorder, eating disorders, schizophrenia, and suicidal thoughts. As Kay Warren wrote, "Chains of hopelessness were broken, and walls of stigma, misunderstanding, confusion, and prejudice began to melt away in the face of recognition, acceptance, and love. People began asking the questions they had been reluctant to ask before: Can a Christian experience a mental illness? . . . Is it okay to take medication for a mental illness?"[10]

Mental illness is common, but it is still an uncomfortable topic —especially as it relates to our children. Sixteen percent of American youth aged six to seventeen experienced a mental health disorder in 2016. Suicide is the second leading cause of death among people aged ten to thirty-four in the United States.[11] According to the Centers for Disease Control, deaths by suicide among ten to twenty-four-year-olds increased 56 percent from 2007 to 2017. For the youngest group, the ten to fourteen-year-olds, the rate almost tripled to about five hundred suicide deaths in 2017. The rise in rates for the entire group has been faster in recent years.[12] Strong community ties provide a source of social support, which is a key protective factor against suicide, but many kids are not growing up in tight-knit communities.

Think of your kids. Do they have a close relationship with you, extended family, and friends? Do they attend church regularly and enjoy the company of others? If they need medical attention or counseling, are they getting it? Are they part of a group like a sports team, band, or service group? As Dr. Henry Cloud says, "The power of being in the physical presence of another person delivers real benefits."[13]

EMOTIONAL SUPPORT PARENT

You've probably seen "emotional support" dogs or other pets. They can provide valuable companionship, but the primary role for providing emotional support shouldn't rest on the shoulders of a well-trained canine. It really rests on the shoulders of a parent. We are the ones, the first responders, who provide emotional support and guidance for our kids.

Emotional growth is progressive, just like physical growth. Kids have emotions very early in life, but they don't have names for those feelings. When they cry because you leave the room, they don't know what to call that emotion, but they know how to express it! We are designed to be emotional creatures. As our children grow, we want to help them name those feelings. Let's say your child starts crying because he wants Daddy, but Daddy is on a business trip. You can say, "You are feeling lonely because the person you want to be with is not here." Coach your child to say something like "I feel lonely tonight without my dad," and then you can pray together or call Daddy on the phone later on. When you give names to emotions and identify them, it helps kids to understand what they are feeling . . . and what others are feeling.

When you give names to emotions and identify them, it helps kids to understand what they are feeling . . . and what others are feeling.

When you watch a movie together, have a conversation afterward that goes something like this: "What do you think the main character was feeling? Why did he get so angry? Why was the little girl crying? Who responded well and who didn't?" You can make watching a movie a learning experience by focusing on what people were feeling and doing in various parts of the film. You want to choose movies that portray positive emotions or negative consequences when people lash out in anger or act in cruel ways.

Emotionally healthy people acknowledge they have feelings, both negative and positive. The key is they learn how to respond to those emotions, and how to handle them. They don't let their emotions control their behavior. This maturity is a lifelong process. The more we can talk about this with our children in the earlier years, the better.

There's a built-in time every day to connect to your child's heart and emotions, and it's triggered by the stomach. Research shows that eating meals as a family benefits children greatly. Young people whose families routinely eat meals together spend more time on homework and reading for pleasure. They are more likely to eat nutritious food and less likely to engage in future substance use, sexual intercourse, or suicidal tendencies.[14]

What you do during the meal is hugely important. Is the television on? Are you quickly gobbling up your food to get out the door? If so, you are missing out on the value of family mealtime. Having a meal together is a time for *conversation*. These sacred moments around the table can draw your quiet child out. If it's dinnertime, you can ask your child questions like "What did you enjoy most today?" or "If you could snap your fingers and change something at school, what would it be?" It's amazing what you can learn sitting around the table, if you will listen.

A *Wall Street Journal* article titled "The Benefits of Retelling Family Stories" emboldens us parents to share our wild or inspiring family tales. Stories provide context and invite children to belong. Even if your kids look uninterested, they absorb more than most adults think. In a study by researchers at Emory, they quizzed children ages ten to fourteen on twenty family history questions, such as: How did your parents meet? Where did your grandparents grow up? Those who answered more questions correctly showed, on separate assessments, less anxiety and fewer behavior problems.[15]

Remember to put your phones on vibrate and don't pick up during mealtime. Turn the television and radio off unless it's just soft music in the background. Don't allow the interruptions of screens to compromise your quality time together. Show your children that dinner is not only a time to eat—it's a time to talk.

With competing schedules, it can be challenging to find a common time when every member of the family can sit down for a meal. One son might have football practice, while another is taking piano lessons, and you are running around town like a professional shuttle service. I (Gary) remember when we had to bounce back and forth from eating early to eating late because of the kids' schedule or my schedule. But we all knew that family dinner was important, and we strove to make it work.

We suggest making it a family goal to eat seven or more meals together a week. Depending on what works with your family's schedule, that might be dinner every night, or most meals on the weekend with a few meals during the week. There might be a night where you have to eat fast food in the car on the way to the game, but make that the exception, not the rule.

Social contact is a core human need for all us, regardless of age. You can fight against loneliness and anxiety one meal at a time, one conversation at a time, so your child will find comfort daily in the presence of family.

We, the grown-ups, need that comfort too, whether we admit it or not. And basically, we all, adults and kids, need places we can just . . . be ourselves. And be accepted. Starting around our tables. If all our kids are doing is scrolling through social media, they aren't getting the interpersonal connection they need. They want to be hugged and spoken to, not texted. They want to laugh at a funny story, not be all anxious about "building their brand." As we meet their emotional needs at home, they'll go into a broken world better prepared to mend it.

5

Screen Time and the Single Parent

We are all faced with a series of great opportunities brilliantly disguised as impossible situations.
—CHUCK SWINDOLL

Shana, nine, sits on the concrete with her backpack next to her. After-school care is over; she sees her mom and hops in the car. After dinner, Shana finishes her homework and starts watching videos. She watches for a few hours, feeling neither happy nor sad. This is her ritual every night until bedtime. But it hasn't always been this way.

She used to curl up with her mom on the sofa to read a story, or take a bike ride around the block with her dad. But since her parents got divorced last year, Shana lives with her mom and sees her dad on the weekends. Her mom is usually tired after work, so Shana learned not to ask her to play or read to her anymore. She misses the way her family used to be.

Because so many children are living in single-parent homes, we want to address some of the needs of these families especially pertaining to screen time. The single mother or father trying to meet the needs of children while at the same time maintaining a career and some semblance of a personal life knows the tensions on the home front. If this is your situation, you know all too well the time pressures, economic demands, and loneliness you and your children have experienced. You have doubts about whether you can do an adequate job of parenting. Many times, you feel overwhelmed at the thought of doing everything yourself.

When your child asks to watch more television or play a video game for another thirty minutes, you know that gives you more uninterrupted time to answer emails, clean the kitchen, or enjoy some needed peace and quiet. The screen becomes a very convenient companion to your child, keeping her occupied and out of trouble. Many single parents can't afford extracurricular activities, nor do they have the time or energy to drive their kids all over town. Television, video games, and YouTube are the easiest ways to pass the time.

FILLING THE VOID?

In the hearts of children whose parents divorce, hurt and anger often run deep and linger long. Children who have lost a parent through death or divorce need time to grieve. While a child is in this emotional state, he often fills the void with video games, movies, virtual worlds, or online communities. Yet excessive screen time is more likely to make a child's emotional problems deepen, not subside. According to the Mayo Clinic[1], too much screen time has been linked to:

Obesity—The more television your child watches, the greater his risk of becoming overweight. Children are not only sedentary while watching; they are bombarded with advertisements for junk food. In addition, kids often snack mindlessly while they watch television.

Irregular sleep—Children who watch a lot of television are more likely to have trouble falling asleep or to have an irregular sleep schedule. Lack of sleep can lead to attention problems in school, fatigue, and overeating.

Behavioral problems—Elementary students who spend more than two hours a day watching TV or using a computer are more likely to have social, emotional, and attention-related difficulties.

Loss of social skills—Elementary students who have a television in their bedroom tend to be outperformed by their peers who don't have screens in the room.

Violence—When a child is exposed to violent video games or television, he becomes desensitized to violence. As a result, children might accept violent behavior as a suitable way to deal with problems.

Less time for play—If children use their free time for computers and television, they will have less time for active, creative play.

It's important to note that these negative effects of excessive screen use can be experienced by *any* child, whatever their family situation. But when a child is having emotional turmoil for whatever reason, they are even more vulnerable to the harms of screen overuse.

REDUCING SCREEN TIME, PROTECTING ME TIME

Most single parents are working full-time to support the family and they are physically exhausted by the end of the day. There's no question that a single parent will struggle with having enough energy to do it all—married parents do too, and when you're the only one "doing it all," it's that much harder. Yet it's important that parents don't succumb to nonstop videos, games, and screen time just because they are too tired to engage with their children.

How does a single parent reduce screen time for a child while still protecting the "me time" he or she desperately needs? One of the best things a parent can do is set an early bedtime for the children. When you put your child to bed early, he learns there is a bedtime and will adjust to that routine. If your child isn't ready to fall asleep that early, you can say, "You don't have to go to sleep right away, but you have to go to your room and be quiet. You can read a book for a few minutes until you go to sleep." This means that the single parent has some time at the end of the day to be alone, to breathe deeply, and to do all the things that need to be done around the home without being interrupted by a child.

If at all possible, an early bedtime is a good idea for children in single-parent *and* two-parent homes. My (Gary's) grandkids routinely went to bed at 8:00 pm in elementary and middle school. They could read in their rooms before going to sleep, but they knew at 8:00 pm, it was time to settle down. My (Arlene's) kids go to bed at 8:30 pm, even my high schooler who is up early for school. My older kids probably read for thirty minutes and then doze off.

Children do what they are trained to do. When a single parent trains her children to go to bed early, it gives that parent the time she desperately needs to take care of herself—plus the sleep is healthy for the children.

In addition to establishing an early bedtime, single parents must evaluate how much time each day is devoted to screen time. If your child is watching more than two hours of videos or playing video games every day, you can work on a plan to reduce his or her screen time. You might begin with these simple action steps:

- Decide what programs your child can watch in advance. Be present when the program is over to turn off the screen before the next video plays automatically.

- Don't use the TV as background noise.
- Make a screen time chart for the week. Mark how much screen time your child has each day and have him check it off once he uses it. Decide if the time carries over if he doesn't use it.
- You may want to have certain days of the week, like weekends, that are used for video games or television days while the rest of the week is media-free.
- Don't allow eating while in front of the TV or computer. Eventually your child will get hungry and will shift gears.

Talk with your child about why you are making these screen time adjustments. Discuss the benefits of having less screen time and more play time or reading time. Your child will probably resist at first, but remember that eventually he will thank you for getting his screen time use under control.

DIFFERENT PARENTS, DIFFERENT RULES

Zack is a hyper six-year-old who loves playing video games. When he is at his dad's house on the weekends, he can play as much as he wants. He and his dad play video games for hours together. But during the week at his mom's house, Zack is only allowed to play games for one hour per day.

"Mom," Zack complains. "Why can't I play more like I do at Dad's house? I can't wait to go back to Dad's."

Zack's mom has explained there are different rules at Dad's house and at her house. Naturally, she feels frustrated by her ex-husband's more lenient screen time rules, and Zack feels frustrated because he can't have what he wants.

In one-parent homes that result from divorce, some children like Zack have ongoing contact with the noncustodial parent. Others suffer from negative contact or a total lack of relationship. When two adults are co-parenting like Zack's mom and dad, they ideally will come together on what the screen time rules are going to be, making them as congruent as possible for the sake of the child.

If Zack's mom prohibits video games while his dad offers unlimited game time, Zack is going to get whiplash going back and forth between those settings. But it is reasonable for Zack's mom to set limits and say something like, "At our house, we are going to play one hour a day. I can't control your father. He's your father. Obviously he is going to do whatever he thinks is best for you. But I'm your mother, and I have to do what I think is best for you."

Sometimes a mother and a father are very antagonistic towards each other. Even then, it would be worth it for a single mom or dad to suggest getting together to set media guidelines that would work in both homes. You may want to get a counselor or pastor to sit down with you to help work out similar guidelines. Sometimes this will be a success, and other times no compromises will be reached because one parent is uncooperative. But it is always worth it to try for the sake of your child.

The noncustodial parent is often tempted to shower a child with gifts like video games or a tablet, perhaps from the pain of separation or feelings of guilt over leaving the family. When these gifts are overly expensive, ill-chosen, and used as a comparison with what the custodial parent can provide, they are really a form of bribery, an attempt to buy the child's love. They may also be a subconscious way of getting back at the custodial parent.

If a child has conservative screen limits with one parent, but a generous allowance of screen time with the other parent, no wonder a child prefers going to the home where the fun is. A child can display anger at the stricter parent, but in time will realize that it was the stricter parent who truly cared. As children get older, they often recognize that their noncustodial parent was using gifts and being overly permissive to manipulate them and earn their favor.

When a divorced couple can work together to raise their children with similar values and media guidelines, the children respond well.

Screen-Smart Single Dad: Jake's Story

Jake is a single dad of two energetic boys: Landon, age seven, and Dylan, age nine. A few years ago, Jake's wife died in a tragic accident. The family is adjusting to this new normal with the help of extended family and friends. For the boys, summer means traveling out of state to visit Grandma for two months.

At Grandma's, the boys are allowed to watch hours of television and play video games as much as they want during their free time, something they are not allowed to do at home. The boys went to summer camps and had plenty of outdoor activities, but they were spending up to five hours a day in front of a screen.

When they got home from the summer at Grandma's, Landon and Dylan were glued to the television. Jake thought to himself, "No way. My kids are not going to be glued to screens after school."

He announced a bold plan to his boys. "For one month, we are not going to watch television, movies, or video games. When the month is complete, we'll celebrate by going to an amusement park."

The boys didn't complain at first because they wanted to go to the amusement park. Instead of watching TV after school, the boys read books. Imagine Jake's delight when he found his boys glued to books instead of the screen. Some mornings, Jake would even find the kids awake at 6:00 am reading.

After a few weeks, his oldest son Dylan said, "I'm glad we're doing this because books are a lot better than television." Of course, the month had its difficulties too, like when Jake wanted to watch the football game or take the boys to a new movie on a weekend and couldn't. But for the most part, the month-long media fast was a breath of fresh air and elevated reading in their home.

When the month ended, however, the boys quickly went back to their television watching. "It's so easy to go back," sighed Jake. The boys have daily limits of watching one hour in the morning before school and one hour after school. They can also earn bonus points if they don't watch TV on weekdays, and those bonus points translate into earning more allowance.

Jake has this advice for single parents: "Don't use television as a crutch. Your kids can have books, games, or toys, and they will gravitate to these other things. Your kids may complain, but just say, 'Sorry, we're not turning on the TV.' They may throw a tantrum for a week, but then they'll adjust. You have to be willing to invest in them."

FILLING YOUR CHILD'S TANK EVEN WHEN YOURS IS EMPTY

Filling your son or daughter's love tank can seem impossible at times. You are exhausted, your child is demanding, and you may feel that you need love yourself. The needs of children in single-parent homes are the same as of children from two-parent homes. It is the *way* that these needs are met that changes; one parent is the primary caregiver instead of two. And the caregiver, whether single through divorce, death, or never being married, is usually wounded.

The children are also hurting. The most common emotions among these children are fear, anger, and anxiety. Movies, television, video games, and virtual worlds rarely bring healing in these areas. It's more likely that excessive or inappropriate screen time will magnify these negative emotions. Some children can move through these stages of grieving more quickly if significant adults in their lives seek to openly communicate with them about their loss. They need someone to talk with and cry with.

Unfortunately, screen time prevents this deep communication from happening and can delay a child's healing process because they never take the time to grieve. Digital distractions delay the pain, and years later, those feelings of fear, anger, and anxiety frequently surface. Listening more, talking less, helping your child face reality, acknowledging hurt, empathizing with pain—all are part of the healing process. But these things cannot happen via text or instant messaging.

If you are aware of your child's primary love language, your efforts at meeting his emotional needs will be more effective. For instance, Robbie's love language was physical touch. His father left when he was nine years old. Looking back, Robbie says, "If it had not been for my granddaddy, I'm not sure I would have made it. The first time I saw him after my father left, he took me in his arms and held me for a long time. He didn't say anything, but I knew he loved me and would always be there for me. Every time he came to see me, he hugged me, and when he left, he did the same thing. I don't know if he knew how much the hugs meant to me, but they were like rain in the desert for me.

"My mom helped a lot by letting me talk and by asking me questions and encouraging me to share my pain. I knew she loved me, but in the early stages, I wasn't willing to receive her love," Robbie admitted. "She would try to hug me and I'd push her away. I think I blamed her for my father leaving. It wasn't until I found out that he left for another woman that I realized how I had misjudged her. Then I started receiving her hugs and we became close again." Learning to fill your child's love tank while your own is running low may seem difficult. But, like Robbie's mother, the wise parent will come to understand what her child uniquely needs—and seek to meet that need.

If you've ever flown in an airplane, you've heard the flight attendant instruct you to put on your own oxygen mask before assisting your child with their oxygen mask in case of emergency. Don't discount your own emotional need for love, because it is just as real as your child's need. Because that need can no longer be met by a former spouse or by a child, the single parent must learn to reach out to friends and family members for support.

FINDING COMMUNITY

No parent can single-handedly meet a child's need for love. This is where grandparents and other extended family members, as well as church and community resources, come into play. Extended family members are always important, but they become even more crucial when children suffer losses and life is unstable. Nearby grandparents can help the grandchildren in several ways during the school week, and their presence can cheer their own single-parent son or daughter. They take some of the emotional burden off the single parent.

No parent can single-handedly meet a child's need for love.

Of course, this is not always possible. Your nearest family member may be hundreds of miles away. If you are a single parent, don't wait until people ask if they can help. Some may be holding back, not wanting to interfere in your family. Others may not be aware of your situation. If you or your children need help, you may want to investigate the resources available in your community. Someone at your child's school or your church may be able to guide you in your search. The more exposure your children have to positive role models, the better.

Being a single parent is one of the toughest assignments out there. Alice, who has been divorced for several years, depended on her son for love and acceptance. She poured her life into him and never crossed him because she feared his disapproval. As her son grew into a teenager, he became consumed with video games, and his mother never corrected him, even though his schoolwork was suffering. She needed her son to like her because it gave her the love and acceptance she desperately craved.

This is one example of why single parents must have strong friendships outside of the home, so they are not dependent on their children to meet their emotional needs. Although a single parent can connect with friends online through social networking, fulfilling relationships need to be nurtured face-to-face or voice-to-voice over the phone. Too many adults are relying on texts and tweets to stay connected to others, and it's simply not enough. Many single moms spend hours on social media and never really connect with anyone in a meaningful way.

As a parent, you have the greatest influence in your child's life. The way you handle your singleness, with dignity and wisdom, can be a source of tremendous strength for your child. You can help restore your child's sense of security, not by the companionship of screens, but with your companionship and the friendship of others.

PART 2

The A+ Social Skills

6

The A+ Skill of Affection

Affection is responsible for nine-tenths of whatever solid and durable happiness there is in our natural lives.
—C. S. LEWIS

In the following chapters, we will outline the five skills every child needs in a tech-driven world. Although academic As are certainly desirable, we believe these A+ skills are even more helpful to predict your child's success in life.

More than anything, Ben wants to be a good father. He's home every night by 6:00 pm. After dinner, he sits on the couch with his children, Megan, eight, and Ryan, nine. He checks the news, views his stocks, and starts reading an article on the best slopes for skiing in the United States on his phone. He's thinking of teaching the kids over Christmas break. Ben is sitting with his kids on the couch while they watch television. But mentally, he's someplace else. He's physically present but his mobile device is his focus. It's the object of his affection.

A subtle shift is happening in our homes. Parents and children alike are growing more comfortable with spending increasing amounts of time with our devices. Unknowingly we've accepted a trade-off. We're becoming less affectionate toward each other and more affectionate with our devices, holding them near at all times. Phones are like new babies. We coddle them. When they make a sound, we come running. We might be sharing the same space as our family members, but we are giving more physical attention and affection to our phones.

STILL THE WINDOW TO THE SOUL

Someday far into the future, your son or daughter may get married. When you think of an idyllic proposal, texting "marry me?" probably doesn't come to mind. Yet young people are texting more, talking less, using their phones more than their faces to connect. The screen world is becoming the real world, and that's especially dangerous when it comes to affection. Any relationship based on texting is malnourished. Physical presence and particularly eye contact is needed to express affection most powerfully.

When my (Arlene's) husband, James, and I were dating, he looked deeply in my eyes one day and asked, "Do you know what I see when I look in your eyes?"

"What do you see when you look in my eyes?" I asked dreamily.

"AV, I see the letters AV. Your contact lens say AV!"

Later that day, I popped out my lenses and indeed they had the letters AV on them. I couldn't believe that James could see that!

We often talk about people looking into each other's eyes for hours when they are falling in love. Husbands and wives should continue to look into one another's eyes long after the wedding ceremony, and the same is true for children and parents. It's healthy for children to watch their parents making eye contact with each other, hugging, kissing, holding hands. It brings security to a child when his parents are affectionate with each other.

When you look at a person's eyes, there's a sense you are looking into their soul. Sight is a precious gift. The next time you are with your child, try looking at your child's arm or foot while you're talking to him. Then fix your attention on his face and look into the eyes. See the difference? You can use this exercise to illustrate the value of eye contact to your child.

Children need eye contact to develop the parts of the brain involved with attachment. Without eye contact, kids grow up disconnected from others, lacking empathy. Psychiatrist Daniel Siegel sums up what a moment of eye contact accomplishes: "Repeated tens of thousands of times in the child's life, these small moments of mutual rapport serve to transmit the best part of our humanity—our capacity for love—from one generation to the next."[1]

Children need eye contact to develop the parts of the brain involved with attachment.

These small moments of eye contact are disappearing because we are relying increasingly on our devices to communicate. How many of us have texted a teenager while both of you were home because it was the quickest way to communicate? Sure, there are some things that texting is great for, like "I'm parked by the main entrance" or "I'm on my way." But the bulk of parenting is best done face-to-face with direct eye contact. You can't look a child in the eye through a text. You can't tell for certain if your child is anxious, disturbed, discouraged, or tired. You can't hug a child through the cellphone. You can't properly instruct a child in a tweet. The eyes are the window to your child's soul. Look into them often and don't always be in a rush to get to the next thing on your agenda. Just lingering for a few seconds, looking in your child's eyes, can make a big difference in the level of affection they feel from you.

Eye contact isn't just important at home. It's important everywhere else. Jocelyn Green, co-author of *The 5 Love Languages Military Edition,* says:

> One thing I have noticed with youth is the lack of eye contact. Even when I buy something at the drugstore, the checkout clerk can do the entire transaction without ever looking at me. It's alarming because I believe it's symptomatic of our screen-oriented relationships. That's why my husband and I are very deliberate in coaching our children to look people in the eyes, observe body language, and respond to questions when they are asked.[2]

Making eye contact with another person used to be considered a common courtesy. Now it will set your child apart from others if they learn this basic skill.

FILLING THE LOVE TANK: THE FIVE LOVE LANGUAGES

Every child has a love tank, a place of emotional strength that can fuel him through the challenging days of childhood and adolescence. There are five ways children (indeed, all people) speak and understand emotional love. If you have several children in your family, chances are they speak different languages. So how does technology impact the way you express love to your child? Here is a brief explanation of each love language. To learn more about showing affection through speaking your child's love language, we recommend you read *The 5 Love Languages of Children.*

Love Language #1: Physical Touch

Bob has two children in elementary school and one in preschool. When the two older kids were younger, Bob would often put them in his lap and read them a bedtime story. Reading together builds a sense of oneness, a sense of love for kids. But life got busier and nowadays, the older kids read on their own and his youngest daughter Lisa, four, is used to reading children's books on an e-reader. Bob rarely puts Lisa on his lap to read *Goodnight Moon*. She sits by herself on the couch reading with her device.

An electronic reader may save space and trees, and be convenient, but using one with kids short-circuits something important—physical touch between a parent and child. Sure, a parent can put a child on his lap and read an e-reader or play a video game together on a tablet. But typically, when a child is engaged with a screen, he or she is not touching a parent. When family members get used to engaging with screens, they lose the physical touch dynamic which should be a normal dynamic in a healthy family.

If your child's primary love language is touch, you will know it. They will be jumping on you, poking you, and constantly trying to sit beside you. I (Arlene) know my youngest daughter Lucy has physical touch as her primary love language because at the age of two, her favorite word was "Huggie!" Physical touch communicates love in a powerful way to all children, not just young children. Throughout elementary school, middle school, and high school, your child still has a strong need for physical touch. A hug given as he leaves each morning may be the difference between emotional security and insecurity throughout the day. Older boys tend to be responsive to more vigorous contact such as wrestling, playful hitting, bear hugs, high fives, and the like. Girls like this type of physical touch also, but they like the softer touches of hugs and holding hands. Screens can't do any of these things, no matter how advanced they are.

Love Language #2: Words of Affirmation

With the rise of screen time, many children are hearing more words from their screens than in actual conversation with family members. A child isn't going to get many meaningful words of affirmation from a television or tablet. Even if he wins a video game and sees the screen flash, that can't be equated with hearing someone you care about say "Well done!"

There's very little a device can do to provide words of affirmation, unless it's a parent using it to speak or text words of affirmation to his or her child. Maybe when your older child is walking home from school, you can text "Your smile makes my day. Love you. See you soon!" Technology can play a role in delivering positive words to your child, but obviously it shouldn't be limited to that. Sometimes a preoccupation with screens on the part of the parent or child can stop that flow of affirming words to a child's heart.

Kids who thrive on words of affirmation also shrivel under criticism or condemnation. Cruel words shared on social media or texts are potentially devastating. That's why it's essential for parents to diminish the input of screens and instead focus on speaking life into their children.

Speak words of affirmation to your child each day. Here are some examples to get you started:

If I could choose any child in the world, I would choose you.

I noticed (insert a specific improvement), and I'm proud of your efforts.

I woke up this morning and thought, "What a privilege it is to be your father/mother."

I enjoy it when you're around.

You handled that situation very well.

You are a hard-working, excellent student.

Love Language #3: Quality Time

Six-year-old Nathan taps on his mother's arm. "Mommy, will you play a game with me?"

"I can't play right now," Lauren says. "I have to finish answering my emails. Maybe in a half hour, okay?"

Fifteen minutes later, Nathan is back and wondering if his mom is finished with her emails. "No, I'm not done yet. Please stop bugging me. I'll let you know when I'm finished."

The chances are good that Nathan was revealing his primary love language—quality time. What really makes him feel loved is his mother's undivided attention. It's very difficult to have quality time with a child when screens are present. Sadly, in many homes, children would miss their iPads and other devices more than they would miss their father or mother. That's because the bulk of their time is spent playing video games, watching videos, or texting friends. Children are more and more influenced by forces outside the family, yet they need the strengthening influence of quality time with their parents. When you spend quality time with your children, it's not just about *doing* things together. Quality time is a means for *knowing* your child better.

Quality time is a means for *knowing* your child better.

Love Language #4: Gifts

You might be inclined to think that every child has the primary love language of gifts, judging from the way they beg for things. It's true that all children want to have more and more, but those whose language of love is receiving gifts will respond differently when they get a gift. They will always make much of receiving the gift. They will want the present to be wrapped, or at least given in a unique and creative way. Often they will ooh and ahh as they open the gift. It will seem like a big deal to them—and it is. They want your undivided attention as they open the gift. Once they have opened the gift, they will hug you or thank you profusely.

The digital age has put gift giving on steroids. Parents and grandparents may need to give less rather than more, carefully choosing gifts that will be meaningful and not harmful. You can ask the following questions when evaluating whether or not to purchase an electronic device or video game for your child:

What message(s) does this device or game communicate to my child?

Are these messages ones with which I am comfortable?

What might my child learn from playing with this device or game?

Will its overall effect tend to be positive or negative?

Is this device or game something we can afford?

Don't allow advertising or popular culture to convince you that you have to buy expensive gifts like the latest tablets and smartphones for your child.

Love Language #5: Acts of Service

If service is your child's primary love language, your acts of service will communicate most deeply that you love him or her. When you fix a bicycle chain, mend a dress, cook a favorite meal, or help with homework, your child's love tank fills up. Your children also need to experience your caring acts of service so they can be taught by example to show concern for others. In the Chapman family, we had an open house every Friday night for college students years ago. We'd pack in twenty to sixty students.

The format was simple: From 8:00 to 10:00 p.m. we had a discussion about a relational, moral, or social issue, drawn from a Bible passage. Next came refreshments and informal conversation. At midnight we kicked them out.

Our children, Shelley and Derek, were young during those years and wandered in and out of the meetings. Often on Saturday mornings, some of the students would return for "Do-Good Projects" like raking leaves for the elderly, or other jobs that needed to get done. Shelley and Derek always went along on these service projects, even though they jumped in the leaves more than they raked them.

We are convinced that sharing our home with others and involving the children at a young age in service had a profound and positive effect in their lives. Make it your goal that your children will learn to be comfortable in serving others. Your children will not pick this up by accident or online. Rather, they will learn it by watching you serve them and other people with joy.

5 Tech-Free Ways to Speak the Love Languages

1. Stroke your child's hair or rub their back when they tell you about a difficult day or are upset (physical touch).

2. Put a Post-it note in their lunchbox with some encouraging words (words of affirmation).

3. When taking your younger children to the park or playground, spend time actually playing with them

instead of watching from a bench or sitting with your phone (quality time).

4. Keep a small collection of inexpensive gifts packed away and give them one at a time as you sense there is a reason to celebrate (gifts).

5. Wake up a half-hour earlier to make a special surprise breakfast for your children (acts of service).

There are some children who don't feel loved by their parents, not because the parents don't love them but because they are not getting enough love in their love language. These children tend to be lethargic and more apt to withdraw from people. In today's world, the natural place to withdraw is screen time with a tablet, television, game console, or phone. The technology itself isn't to blame; the screen is simply the modern place for a child to withdraw when they don't feel loved by their parents.

Many parents welcome screens into their home because it keeps the children occupied and they don't want their children to "fall behind" technologically. But perhaps more importantly, parents must realize that a child can fall behind emotionally . . . and it's possible for a child to fall behind to such an extent that he can never catch up.

As you learn how to consistently speak the five languages of love to your child—physical touch, words of affirmation, quality time, receiving gifts, and acts of service—you are giving your child the affection he or she desperately needs to thrive. What you do in loving your children will show the world that the language of love isn't most powerfully spoken in pixels or posts, but by parents.

Parents have a daily golden opportunity to show real affection to our children—face-to-face. It might be given through a hug, conversation, clearing the dishes together, or going on a special trip to the ice cream shop. Your presence means a great deal to your child, and not just your physical presence but your mental and emotional presence.

Older kids may not be as vocal as young ones, but the need for affection is equally important. Especially against the electronic background of screens surrounding us, our kids must feel our love and affection in a real way. Otherwise, the temptation to look for affection in the wrong places becomes too strong. However, with your guidance, your child can learn how to give and receive affection in the way God intended: through healthy human relationships.

7

The A+ Skill of Appreciation

Gratitude is not only the greatest of virtues, but the parent of all the others.

—ATTRIBUTED TO CICERO

Jesse waits with a bunch of rowdy third graders in the lunch line. The cafeteria worker puts milk, chicken nuggets, apple slices, and a cookie on his tray. He takes his tray and walks toward a long table, without a word of thanks or even making eye contact with the lady.

It's Christmas Day and Sarah can't wait to open her gift. She tears the paper off the small box. "We hope you like it," Sarah's mom says with a big smile. The box opens to reveal a shiny white phone. "Oh no," Sarah sighs with disappointment. "I wanted the *latest* one!"

We live in an age of entitlement where the simple words "thank you" are rare. Author Kristen Welch writes in her book, *Raising Grateful Kids in an Entitled World*: "Entitlement winds its course through my home, and the more I've become aware of its subtle infiltration, the more I see and hear it blatantly. *This is all I get? There's nothing else?* From ice cream serving sizes to allowances, the opportunity to demand more is present. *Is that all?* I believe these three little words sum up the tone for those of us in most Western cultures."[1]

In this world of instant everything, children can grow accustomed to being served exactly what they want, on demand, with no waiting.

Being raised on technology has made things worse. There are thousands of video options to stream on demand. Your child doesn't have to wait one week to watch another episode of her favorite program. She can watch four episodes in a row. When bored with a video game, there's always a new one to play. If you order something on Amazon, it could be on your doorstep tomorrow. In this world of instant everything, children can grow accustomed to being served exactly what they want, on demand, with no waiting. Alexa, play this song. Alexa, open Netflix. Alexa, turn lights off. Do you think any child ever says, *Alexa, thank you*?

STOPPING TO SAY THANKS

There is a Bible story found in Luke chapter 17 about ten men with the disease of leprosy who were healed by Jesus. Pronounced clean of their contagious condition, which had trapped them as social outcasts, they were able to reenter society and see their loved ones again. What a life-changing reason to be thankful, yet only one man—a Samaritan, a foreigner, returned to express gratitude. Jesus asked, "Didn't I heal ten men? Where are the other nine? Has no one returned to give glory to God except this foreigner?"

Maybe you've felt a little like this after hosting a children's party. One angelic child says "thank you," and you wonder, "Didn't I feed twenty, yet only one child says thank you?" Hofstra University associate professor Jeffrey Froh, PsyD is a pioneering researcher of gratitude in youth. He and his team tested a new type of "gratitude curriculum" for elementary school children ages eight to eleven. Kids learned about three types of considerations that make us feel grateful:

- that someone has intentionally done something to benefit us.
- that providing this benefit was costly to them.
- that the benefit is valuable to us.

After one week of daily half-hour lessons on gratitude, the students showed significant increases in grateful thinking and mood. You go where you focus. When given the choice to write a thank-you note to the PTA, the students who received the gratitude lessons wrote 80 percent more notes than the students who did not receive the lessons. Five months after the curriculum was taught, students who were in the gratitude group showed steady increases in grateful thinking and positive emotions, showing the lessons had staying power.[2]

You can create your own gratitude curriculum at home by reading Bible stories, newspaper or magazine articles, and short classic stories, and then highlighting gratitude. Ask questions like: What did that character do to benefit someone else? What did it cost that character to give that gift or act in kindness? How did that sacrifice benefit someone else?

When my (Arlene's) children receive a gift, we make it a habit to send a thank-you note. But since reading about Dr. Froh's gratitude curriculum, I'm trying to take it one step deeper by pausing to consider the giver. For example, my kids received coupons for free ice cream from their aunt. Naturally, ice cream is cause for celebration, but before moving on, I asked the kids to consider what it cost their aunt to send this. She had to pick out the coupon, pay for it with her own money, write a note, put a stamp on it, and get it in the mail. That took her time, thought, money, and effort. When the kids plunge their spoons into that free ice cream, a layer of gratitude towards their aunt will make it all the sweeter. As children realize good gifts don't drop effortlessly from the sky, they will learn to be more grateful for the labor that goes into each gift and act of service. This gratitude awareness doesn't come naturally; it must be taught.

THE GRATITUDE MUSCLE

Did you know that gratitude can be worked out and strengthened, like a muscle? A team of researchers from Indiana University recruited forty-three subjects suffering from anxiety or depression. Half of them were told to complete a gratitude exercise and write letters of thanks. They were given the option to mail the letter or not to share it. They spent twenty minutes writing thankful letters once a week for three weeks. That's just one hour total. Those who did the gratitude exercise were more likely to give to charity—and brain scans revealed that those who gave away money showed a particular pattern of activity in their brains.

Months later they still reported feeling more thankful and still showed more gratitude-related brain activity in the scan. This suggests the more you practice being grateful, the more your brain adapts to this reality. You and your children have a gratitude "muscle" that can be exercised and strengthened on purpose.[3]

Dr. Susan Ferguson, a neuroscientist at the Center for Integrative Brain Research at Seattle Children's Research Institute, says,

"Research shows that gratitude is linked with feelings of reward, improved sleep and decreased depression and anxiety. . . . There are measurable benefits to mental health and interpersonal relationships when humans feel gratitude."[4]

Just like your child's physical muscles can weaken by sitting in front of a screen for hours each day, their gratitude muscles can atrophy as well. It's our job to get those "thank-you" muscles moving on a regular basis. Motivational speaker and author Zig Ziglar said it this way: "Gratitude is the healthiest of all human emotions. The more you express gratitude for what you have, the more likely you will have even more to express gratitude for."[5]

FROM "GOT TO" TO "GET TO"

I (Arlene) grew up as an only child. My husband, James, who is the youngest of four, is quick to point out that although I wasn't "spoiled rotten," I was for sure spoiled. The first time I did my own laundry was as a freshman in college. James, on the other hand, was doing his own laundry by second grade.

By participating in household chores, children realize that keeping a house takes effort and they become more appreciative. Following in James' footsteps, our kids are doing laundry, emptying dishwashers, and completing chores around the house. One afternoon I was writing, and my kids, then six and eight, were arguing about who would clean the toilets. But they were actually arguing because they both *wanted* to clean the toilets. Apparently watching the water turn blue and swishing the cleaner around with a brush is actually fun (by the way, they are over it now).

Use every opportunity to turn the "got to's" in life into "get to's." For most of us, cleaning toilets is a "got to," but to my kids years ago it was a "get to." Consider the different attitudes expressed in these two statements: "I have to go to school" and "I get to go to school." Harvard lecturer and author Shawn Achor was invited to go on a speaking tour through Africa. One of the stops was a school next to a shantytown where there was no electricity and hardly any running water. He realized that many of his stories about Harvard and privileged American students would not translate. Trying to find a common point of reference, he asked the group of children, "Who here likes to do schoolwork?" He expected the universal distaste of homework to provide a common bond, but instead he found the opposite. Ninety-five percent of the children raised their hands and smiled enthusiastically.[6] Those children saw schoolwork as a privilege—as a "get to," something their parents never had the chance to achieve. We all have something to learn about gratitude from those schoolchildren.

THE ENEMY OF GRATITUDE: INDULGENCE

Dan's son Maxwell, five, was obsessed with the train set he had seen in the store window. His parents bought the set and wrapped it up for his birthday. When Maxwell saw that train, he exploded with joy. He set it up in the living room and played with it every day for two weeks. After a month went by, the train went unused most days. Now Maxwell had his sights on a helicopter. He talked his parents into buying it for him. Then he begged for a robot, play guitar, and a scooter. His parents grew weary of his nagging and figured buying these things would make Maxwell happy. But instead of being grateful, he just wanted more and more; the more toys he had, the more he wanted. And the less he appreciated them.

When a child is indulged and given unrestrained gratification of his own appetites and desires, he becomes spoiled and selfish. Don't try to make your child happy or rescue him by indulging his whims. You don't need to supply your children with every game and gadget you can afford. The kind of happiness that comes from acquiring things is temporary at best. We do children a great disservice when we give them everything they want. This is not how the real world works.

Even if your child's love language is gifts, you still don't have to give them everything they want.

Many times children will say, "But everyone else has one!" which incidentally is never true. Just because a child says they want something isn't your signal to scramble in order to get it for them. Parents have asked, "What if my child's love language is gifts? Won't they be hurt or feel unloved if I don't get what they want?" Even if your child's love language is gifts, you still don't have to give them everything they want. At times, we will say no to our kids because we know what they are asking for is not going to be helpful to them. Other times we say "wait" because we know they are not ready for it or maybe it's not in the budget.

Children who make their parents feel guilty or like they are bad parents because they don't give them certain things must be challenged early on. Most of us recognize that the younger generation has a strong entitlement mentality. "I deserve that" and "You owe that to me" are attitudes that kids can easily pick up. But the only thing a child is really entitled to is his parent's love. Not to keep up with the Joneses. Not a brand new bike or iPad, but love. If a child has your unconditional love, he has the greatest asset in the world. If we as parents can realize it's love that our children need most, and not things, we will stop trying to buy our children's happiness with possessions.

We can help our children develop a more sensible range of

wants and a deeper appreciation for what they have. Teach your son or daughter to wait for what they want. Sometimes they have to wait until they earn enough money or until they are old enough to have a particular device, video game, or toy. Ultimately they will enjoy that object more if they have waited for it and worked hard to earn it.

The most bored children in the world are teenagers whose parents gave them everything they wanted. There comes a time when there's nothing else they can reach for. Many of them start reaching for forbidden fruit. They get bored with the normal things of life and start experimenting with drugs, sex, or other things that are going to be destructive to them and cause great pain to the family.

There's tremendous value in letting children learn that you have to wait for many things in life. Remember you are raising future adults. That may be hard to keep in mind when you're toting around a diaper bag, but it isn't any less true. If your children grow up with everything they want, what kind of adults will they become? You may know a young couple who buys everything in their first year of marriage that they can't afford and a few years later, they are declaring bankruptcy. They didn't learn how to wait when they were children. They didn't learn how to appreciate what they had.

GRATITUDE THROUGH THE AGES

Nothing is more important in life than knowing how to build positive relationships with people and God. Having a thankful heart serves as the foundation. Maybe you've observed your toddler rant and rave, and you wonder how there can be a thankful heart inside that two-foot-tall tyrant. Are young children capable of showing gratitude and if so, at what age?

There's not an arbitrary age when a switch flips and a child can comprehend and express gratitude. However, rather early on, around age two or three, you can begin to teach children the concept of sharing and saying thank you. There are many good habits you can teach kids very early on—things like saying thank you to a parent at mealtime or after receiving a gift. The sooner you start those expressions of gratitude, the more likely your child is going to connect to doing the kinds of things that build relationships.

Grateful kids realize that the whole world doesn't revolve around their wants and needs. Freshly washed laundry, a hot meal, and a cleaned-up toy room don't just happen automatically. A mom or dad has to work hard to make those things happen. Realizing that someone has gone out of their way to help doesn't come naturally to a child, but they can learn it.

By age two or three, children can talk about being thankful for specific objects, people, pets, and experiences. A toddler can say, "Thank you for the doll" or "That was fun. Thanks!"

By age four, in addition to being thankful for material things like toys, they can express thanks for hugs, affirming words, and other caring acts.

By five or six, kids can write their own thank-you notes with some help from mom or dad. They can give a hug to a loved one, look them in the eye, and express their thanks. They can call a relative who lives far away to say thank you for a birthday gift.

By seven or eight, a child can keep a notebook where they write down a few things they are thankful for each day.

By nine, many children are mature enough to help with a service project with those who are less fortunate. Volunteering in a soup kitchen, for example, can serve as a real eye-opener for kids.

By their tween and teen years, your children can do just about anything you can to show and communicate gratitude to others. They can bake cookies for others, write thank-you letters to teachers and youth leaders, or participate in a short missions trip. When my (Gary's) granddaughter was fourteen, she cooked an entire meal for her family to say "thank you" to her mom and dad for the work they do every day.

Numerous studies prove a variety of positive outcomes of gratitude in adults, including improved physical health, emotional and mental health, and protection from stress and depression. Not surprisingly, the same is true of teenagers. Early adolescents (ages eleven to thirteen) who were grateful reported more optimism, social support from family and peers, and satisfaction with school, family, community, friends, and self than their less grateful counterparts. Grateful late adolescents (ages fourteen to nineteen) reported greater life satisfaction, social integration, absorption in activities, and academic achievements, and less envy, depression, and materialism.[7] Gratitude is also linked to lower levels of aggression. Kids who express thanks are more empathetic towards others, making them less prone to aggression and violent behaviors.[8] You don't have to wait until your children reach a certain age before teaching them about gratitude. All throughout their childhood, you can be modeling a thankful heart and training them how to express thanks in age appropriate ways. These skills will serve them for a lifetime.

Ten Screen-Free Ways to Cultivate a Thankful Heart in Your Child

Scavenger Hunt—Equipped with paper and pen, go through your room and write down all the items you are thankful that you have.

Family Tree—Have your child draw a family tree, complete with parents, grandparents, siblings, aunts, uncles, and cousins. Talk together about positive things you enjoy about each person. Pray and thank God for your family.

Fight Hunger—Volunteer at a food bank to help stock food in a warehouse, assemble bags of food, or distribute food. Talk about your experience over family dinner.

Save Money for a Cause—Sponsor a child through a relief organization, buy a well for a needy family in the developing world, or send toys to a poor family at Christmas. You can keep a jar in a central location so everyone can contribute their loose change and bills. Be creative—maybe you can skip dessert for a week and put the money you save into the jar.

Be a Good Neighbor—Bake cookies or brownies for your neighbors, just because. Attach a note of appreciation: "Thanks for being a great neighbor!" and have your children sign it. Deliver the cookies together and make sure your children see how the neighbors respond.

Paper Chain—Have your children write what they are thankful for on strips of paper. Use the strips to make a gratitude chain and hang it up at home.

Write a Treasured Note—Have your child think of someone important in her life: a teacher, coach, pastor, or relative. Have her complete this sentence in her note: "You have made a difference in my life because ____________________."

Keep a Gratitude Journal—Have your child write up to five things they are grateful for each day. At the end of the week, have your child read the list aloud to the family.

Rice Again?—You can teach your children to appreciate the variety of foods they have by offering them only rice for one day. Don't worry, it's not going to hurt your child for one day, and it will be a memorable lesson on how many children of the world eat every day.

Play "Grateful Hot Potato"—Have your family sit in a circle. It doesn't matter if you use a potato, ball, rolled up socks, or stuffed animal. The object of the game is to say something you are grateful for and then pass the hot potato to the next family member. If you can't come up with anything new to say within five seconds, you're out.

EVERY DAY IS THANKSGIVING

Giving thanks is the star of Thanksgiving Day, but if that's the only time a family verbalizes what they are thankful for, it isn't enough. Gratitude is something children learn best by watching it modeled in everyday life. A father can say to a mother (or vice versa), "I really appreciate your work on putting this meal together. It's delicious." If children constantly hear parents appreciating one another, they will learn to do the same. Look for things to thank your spouse and children for each day. *Thank you for taking out the trash. I really appreciate you sorting out the mail. Thank you for the hug.* If saying "thank you" is a way of life in your home, your child will move into the world always being grateful for what other people do for them.

When you as a parent realize it's your responsibility to model thanksgiving to your child, it changes the way you see the world. You begin to look for blessings, and it becomes easier to notice the hard work of others. I (Arlene) was at a coffeehouse with my kids. I looked at the barista's name—Marissa. I told my kids loud enough so she could hear, "Did you know that Marissa has to know how to make a hundred different drinks and that is a challenging job? She is working hard to make Mommy's coffee just right. Thank you, Marissa!" Marissa's face lit up. My kids were learning to appreciate others and I felt great for making Marissa's day brighter. The giving of thanks blesses everyone involved.

You can teach your children to go against the tide. When others tear down, they can build up. When others concentrate on accumulating more possessions, they can outdo others with acts of generosity. When others are posting gripes and mean comments, they can express appreciation. When others complain about their lives, they can be grateful.

The power of gratitude can change your child's attitude and actions for the better, both in the real world and the digital world. Training your child to think, speak, and text gratefully begins right at home, with the thankful words and actions you model. As G. K. Chesterton wrote, "When it comes to life the critical thing is whether you take things for granted or take them with gratitude."[9]

8

The A+ Skill of Anger Management

Anger is an acid that can do more harm to the vessel in which it is stored than to anything on which it is poured.
—ATTRIBUTED TO MARK TWAIN

Late-night talk show host Jimmy Kimmel issued a YouTube challenge that went viral. Parents were instructed to sneak up on their kids playing the video game *Fortnite* and turn off the TV. The audience gasped and groaned as if to say, "Oh no, you didn't!" The video rolled showing boys yelling at the top of their lungs, rolling around, cursing, falling down, and even striking their parents. Angry boys said things like:

Dad, what are you doing? What is wrong with you? Leave! Go cook!

What the [bleep]???

My friend just died because of you!

Please no!! Stop!!!

As of this writing, that *Fortnite* video has been viewed more than 11 million times.[1] Many parents can attest they don't have to go onto YouTube for that kind of "entertainment." Angry outbursts occur right in the comfort of their own living room when it's time to turn off the video games.

No one has to teach children to experience anger; that happens automatically. Our task is to teach them how to manage their anger. When your child gets angry, don't try to distract him by offering a different video game or his favorite snack. Distractions, delays, or deflections won't help your child learn how to process emotions in a healthy manner.

As I (Gary) talk to parents across the country, most are eager to learn how to help their children in this important area of development. Let me share with you the principles I have shared with many parents in counseling and in parenting workshops. They are simple to understand, but not necessarily easy to do.

PARENTAL GUIDANCE REQUIRED

Just as a child must be taught to tie her shoes or ride a bicycle, so a child must be taught how to handle anger. A child has only two ways to express anger: verbally and behaviorally. Each of these can be positive or negative. Behaviorally, a child may express anger by pushing, shoving, striking, throwing objects, pulling hair, or beating his own head against the wall. Obviously, these are negative behavioral responses to anger. On the other hand, leaving the room, counting to a hundred aloud, or taking a walk outside are mature behavioral responses to anger that allow the child to cool down and process anger in a constructive manner.

On the verbal side, the child may yell and scream condemning statements or may use profanity or name-calling—all very destructive ways of verbalizing anger. But the extremely mature child may acknowledge that he is angry and ask for an opportunity to discuss his complete concerns. Your task as a parent is to take your child where he is and help him move toward more constructive ways of processing anger.

If your child is screaming at you in anger, listen! Calmly ask questions and let the anger be expressed. The more questions you ask and the more intently you listen, the more likely his volume will decrease. Concentrate on the reason your child is angry, not on the way he is expressing it. If he thinks he was wronged, the anger will not go away until he feels that you have heard and understood the complaint.

You may be asking, "Should I let my child yell at me?" Obviously that is not an appropriate way to handle anger. However, at the moment, you want to hear the child's concerns. Later, you can talk about a healthier way to share concerns. Some of us expect our teenagers to be more mature than we ourselves are. I remember the teen who said in my office, "My dad yells and screams at me while telling me to stop yelling and screaming at him." When parents say, "You are not going to talk to me like that. Now shut up and go to your room," they are driving the child's anger underground.

If parents do not hear the child's complaints and seek to understand why the child feels that way, the child's anger will be internalized and later show up in his behavior. Psychologists call this passive-aggressive behavior. The child is passive on the outside, but inside the anger is growing and will eventually express itself in aggressive behavior, such as low grades, drug experimentation, sexual activity, "forgetting" to do homework, or some other behavior that the child knows will upset the parent. If parents understood the extreme danger of passive-aggressive behavior, they would make every effort to listen to their children when they are angry, to hear the issues carefully, to seek to understand, and to find a resolution.

This doesn't mean that the parent must always do what the child is requesting. The child's anger is often distorted, that is, rooted in a perceived wrong rather than a definitive wrong. It's triggered by a disappointment, an unfulfilled desire, something that's been lost, a frustrated effort, or a bad mood; none of which have to do with any genuine wrongdoing. You can help your child to ask two questions to determine the validity of anger. The first is, "What wrong was committed?" And the second is, "Am I sure I have all the facts?"

When your child is angry, you can give him the common sense advice to count to ten (or fifty for older kids) until his anger cools down. Then you ask him to complete the sentence, "I am angry because ________." Seven-year-old Thomas was upset because his younger sister Kayla wrote all over his homework. That was the wrong that was committed. Next you would gather facts together. Did she do it on purpose, or was it an accident? The smirk on her face, followed by a confession, tells you that Kayla did it on purpose. Kayla apologized to Thomas, and her favorite set of markers was taken away for a few days.

Each anger experience gives the parent an opportunity to guide the child through the anger episode, deal with the issues, and find a resolution. Each time this is done, the child becomes a bit more mature in verbalizing his anger. Unfortunately, with increased screen time for both kids and parents alike, many of these teaching opportunities pass by because family members are too busy and distracted to deal with the root of their anger flare-ups. Parental guidance is desperately needed to help children handle anger responsibly.

"Good" Versus "Bad" Anger

"Good" (Definitive)

DEFINITION: Anger toward any kind of genuine wrongdoing; mistreatment, injustice, breaking of laws.

SPARKED BY: Violation of laws or moral code.

HOW TO RECOGNIZE: If you can answer yes to the questions, "Was a wrong committed?" and "Do I have all the facts?"

WHAT TO DO: Either confront the person or decide to overlook the offense.

"Bad" (Distorted)

DEFINITION: Anger toward a perceived wrongdoing where no wrong occurred.

SPARKED BY: People who hurt or irritate us; stress, fatigue; unrealistic expectations.

HOW TO RECOGNIZE: Feelings of frustration or disappointment feed the anger.

WHAT TO DO: Halt the anger, and gather information to process your anger.

WATCH HOW I DO IT

Parents are the most influential persons in developing a child's pattern of anger management. This should encourage us because it gives us an opportunity to give our children positive anger management skills. On the other hand, this can be a frightening reality if we are prone to loud tirades or icy silence. Fortunately, we can learn to change destructive patterns and establish new healthier models of processing anger for ourselves and for our families.

Open conversation, allowing your child to ask questions and make comments, could be a springboard not only for discussing anger as a topic, but also to talk about how you have processed anger in the past, and what positive changes might be made. In such a family conversation, parents might share with a child their own struggles with anger, which creates an atmosphere for a child to express his own struggles or to ask questions.

Such conversations can easily be initiated by sharing with the child something you read recently. For example, "I was reading an article the other day on anger. It said that many parents are not aware of how many times they lose their temper with their children and say things that actually hurt the children, but the parent never remembers what she said. I was wondering if that could possibly be true of me."

"Well, Mom, since you brought it up . . . "

When you make your anger, rather than the child's anger, the focus of the conversation, you make it easier for the child to be responsive and reveal his perceptions of you and the way you handle anger. Such conversations can be extremely instructive to a child, and may also bring insight to the parent.

Reading and discussing Bible stories that focus on anger provides an interesting format for instruction as well. Stories like Cain and Abel, Joseph and his eleven brothers, Jonah and his anger toward God, and Jesus and His anger toward the money-changers all provide key insights into understanding anger.

Memorizing Scriptures is also an excellent method of instruction for children. Consider these verses:

Fools give full vent to their rage, but the wise bring calm in the end.—Proverbs 29:11

Whoever is patient has great understanding, but one who is quick-tempered displays folly.—Proverbs 14:29

"In your anger do not sin": Do not let the sun go down while you are still angry, and do not give the devil a foothold. —Ephesians 4:26–27

For more information on handling your own anger, you can read my (Gary's) book, *Anger: Taming a Powerful Emotion.*

DO VIDEO GAMES FUEL ANGER?

Tony was a typical fifth-grader. He liked sports more than schoolwork but did fine in his class. After soccer practice and homework, he was allowed to play video games. He learned about the video games the sixth-graders were playing and before long, he was playing them too. Even though the rating of the game was for seventeen-year-olds, all of his classmates were playing, so his parents figured it was all right.

But after a few months, his parents noticed a change in Tony. His teacher called because he was being disrespectful to her, as well as fighting with another boy in his class. At home, he had little patience for his little sister and would lash out often. If his parents asked him what was wrong, it would make him angrier.

Was there a connection between playing those mature video games and his negative change in behavior? Probably, according to the 90 percent of pediatricians and 67 percent of parents who agree that violent video games can increase aggressive behavior among children.[2] In fact, more than a thousand studies, including reports from the US Surgeon General's office and the National Institutes of Mental Health, point overwhelmingly to a causal connection between media violence and aggressive behavior in some children.[3]

An experiment conducted in 1961 at Stanford University can help us understand the connection between what we see and how we act. Researcher Albert Bandura used three- and five-foot inflatable plastic toys called Bobo dolls that were weighted, so they would bounce back up to the upright position when knocked down. The research subjects were preschoolers. The Bobo doll was in the room along with a TinkerToy set. One group watched as the researchers abused Bobo the doll by kicking, punching, and throwing him across the room. Researchers made aggressive statements like "Sock him in the nose" and "Pow." Other kids in the control group watched the researchers ignore the Bobo doll and just play with the TinkerToys.[4]

In the final stage, the children's behavior was observed and rated according to the degree of physically and verbally aggressive behavior they exhibited. The children who had been exposed to the aggressive researchers yielded significantly higher levels of aggression. They were much more likely to beat up on the Bobo doll themselves. The effect was stronger when the adult modeling the behavior was the same sex as the child, suggesting that kids were more likely to imitate those they identify with. Albert Bandura's Observational Theory (also known as Social Learning Theory) describes the way people imitate certain behaviors (such as violence) through a process known as modeling.[5] University of Michigan professor L. Rowell Huesmann says it this way: "If you're exposed to violence, you're more likely to catch it." Huesmann suggests that the correlation between media violence and aggression is higher than the correlation between lack of condom use and sexually transmitted HIV, and nearly as high as the correlation between smoking and lung cancer.[6]

It doesn't mean a child will always "catch" becoming angry and violent when watching violent movies or video games. But it does make them more susceptible. Once you start to see violence as a contagious process, you can respond by limiting exposure to violent media to stop its spread in your child's life.

Many people would like to think that violence in video games, movies, and television does not affect children. The reality is that your child is affected by everything he interfaces with. Video games are especially dangerous because a child is not passively watching a violent act. He is participating in it. An international study of more than 17,000 children and adolescents ages nine to nineteen, conducted from 2010 to 2017, found playing violent video games led to increased physical aggression over time. Kids who played violent games such as "Grand Theft Auto" and "Call of Duty" were more likely to be sent to the principal's office for fighting or hitting a non-family member.[7]

Video games are especially dangerous because a child is not passively watching a violent act.

If you realize your child is playing video games that are not healthy, cut back on that game and make it a goal to eliminate violent video games altogether. Replace those video games with more creative ones that do not involve violence, and seek out friends who like to do things besides gaming.

LEARNING TO MANAGE ANGER

When your child is old enough to send a text or email, it's time to teach them what is and what is not appropriate to say online.

You can communicate information, but you cannot use electronics to express anger. It will become a harmful habit that's difficult to break in adulthood if your child learns to use texting or social media to insult others or to get revenge on someone who has made him angry. The ugly words on screens can be read over and over again, making an emotional mark on a child who is not ready. Teach your children to deal with their anger in real life, not on screens.

Just like adults, children need to learn how to manage anger to enjoy close relationships in life. Having a full love tank will certainly assist, as well as getting plenty of sleep and healthy recreation. Kids recharge in outdoor play, settling down with a good book, or hugging and talking to a parent. Relaxation doesn't occur while holding a screen, yet that is how so many children are spending all their free time. Without downtime and visual relaxation, children are more restless and prone to anger. In addition, screen worlds emphasize speed, so a child raised on computers has little patience in real life. As a result, when that child has to wait for something, his impatience can quickly morph into frustration and anger.

You serve as a very important guide to your child. Your kids are watching how you handle your anger. Remember Bobo the doll? Your kids are going to identify with you and imitate you. Parents who display positive changes in how they deal with their own anger will soon see their children improve how they manage their anger too.

If Your Child is Getting Angry Because of a Video Game

Watch for symptoms of anger such as yelling, clenched fists, pounding on the table, swearing, etc.

Take away the controller and divert your child to another activity.

Go outside and get some physical exercise.

Consider the cause of anger

Maybe the game is beyond your child's skill level, causing a lot of frustration. Find a game that is an appropriate skill level.

Play a less violent video game.

Block or avoid other players who make your child angry.

Conversation starters

"We recognize you tend to get angry when you play this game. We are going to give you another game to play instead."

"We made a mistake by letting you play this video game. It is not helping you—you come away frustrated and upset. We're not going to let you play this video game anymore."

Helpful Dialogues for You and Your Angry Child

If your pattern has been to argue with your child, perhaps you can break the pattern by saying,

"I've been thinking about us, and I have realized that I am not a very good listener. Usually when you are feeling strongly about something, I also end up getting mad. I really want to be a better listener. In the future, I am going to try to ask more questions and really seek to understand your feelings. I really do think your ideas and feelings are important."

If your child is pushing, yelling, or throwing things, focus on the anger first and the behavior second.

"It's obvious that you are very angry. I would like to hear what's bothering you, but we can't talk while you are ___________. Would you like for us to take a walk and talk about it?"

If you lose your temper with your child, be willing to confess your failures.

"Son, I'm sorry that I lost my temper this afternoon. I didn't handle my anger well, and the way I talked to you was not kind. Some of the things I said are not really the way I feel. I want you to know that I recognize that was wrong and I have asked God to forgive me; and I want to ask you to forgive me."

9

The A+ Skill of Apology

Never ruin an apology with an excuse.
—ATTRIBUTED TO BENJAMIN FRANKLIN

It had been a tough day in sixth grade for Mia. Her best friend, Jane, who usually ate lunch with her, picked a different table in the cafeteria with three other girls. At the end of lunch, the girls walked up to Mia and said mockingly, "Nice shirt." Her friend just stood there and said nothing. Jane ignored Mia for several days. A few weeks later, Mia's phone buzzed. It was a text message from Jane: "Sorry 4 being mean lately."

Although Mia was relieved to get the text, she wondered why Jane had acted so weird. She felt hurt and betrayed. But she texted back "It's OK," even though in her heart, it really wasn't.

When a girl like Jane texts an apology instead of delivering it in person, she misses the opportunity to grow and mature. She types in "Sorry 4 being mean lately" and hits send. Not much is required to do this. She didn't have to muster the courage to look her friend in the eye and admit she been acting awfully. She doesn't get to feel the sadness that comes from genuine repentance. She doesn't see the hurt in her friend's eyes before the apology and the relief, love, and forgiveness afterwards.

Jane just hits send, and then nothing happens. Online apologies are very different than those given face-to-face.

For the sake of efficiency, convenience, and to save face, we often use our electronic devices to do the work of apologizing for us. In trivial matters, an online apology or text message may work fine for things like "Sorry I 4got to feed cat. Can u do it when u get home?" But when you have offended someone or hurt their feelings like the case with Mia and Jane, a text is clearly not enough.

Unfortunately, many teens are communicating personal messages, such as apologizing, via text. A child can avoid putting herself in a hard and awkward situation with an electronic "sorry." Yet those truncated messages shortchange children emotionally. They grow up unable to have difficult conversations with the people they truly care about. Hiding from stressful situations negatively impacts their ability to interact with people, both now and in the future.

The A+ skill of apology is necessary for healthy relationships, because no one is perfect. We all do things that are hurtful, sometimes on purpose, sometimes on accident. Either way, when we do wrong, we must apologize. And when someone does us wrong and apologizes, we must choose to forgive. This is the way to build healthy relationships, yet many children have never been taught how to offer a sincere apology—or how to accept one.

One of the best ways of teaching this skill is by role modeling what a proper apology looks like. If a child hears her father apologizing to her mother because he raised his voice at her, and then she hears Mom forgive him and they hug, that's a powerful lesson. When that same child gets in a loud fight with her brother, she can remember the example she has seen from her parents. She will learn how to apologize face-to-face with her family first, and then with others outside of the home. Real-life, real-time apologies are extremely important for a child to learn.

5 KEYS TO APOLOGIZING

There are five things you can teach your child about apologizing that will benefit them greatly in life. You might explain to your child they are keys that will open up doors to better friendships and closer family relationships. Add even more interest by telling them that most kids don't have these keys, but that you would like to give these keys to your child. For a younger child you may want to cut out a shape of a key on a piece of construction paper, handing them a paper key as you explain each concept.

Key #1—Accept Responsibility

You can go shopping online and easily find the t-shirt "Sorry Not Sorry." It's available for men, women, and kids in a wide array of colors. What does this message "Sorry Not Sorry" communicate to a child? It could be interpreted in a positive way—for instance if your child stood up for his beliefs against the crowd and proclaimed "Sorry Not Sorry!" But it usually communicates something more like, "You want me to do my homework? I'm going to play instead. Sorry *not* sorry." More often it means the person doesn't really care if his or her behavior upsets someone else. It is the antithesis of accepting responsibility when you hurt someone.

Yet teaching your child how to apologize begins with accepting responsibility for wrongdoing. The natural tendency is to say, with swagger, "Sorry not sorry," or to blame someone else—"It's *his* fault!" A five-year-old can grab a cookie, break it, and throw it on the floor, and then say, "It broke." *It* didn't break. The child broke the cookie. A parent can use that moment to teach this principle of accepting responsibility. "Honey, let's say it a different way–'I broke the cookie.' The cookie didn't break itself, right? You did it. There's nothing wrong with breaking the cookie. You just have to take responsibility for your own actions and not blame the cookie for doing something it can't do." Children can learn to accept responsibility even at a young age. One way to help children learn to accept responsibility for their not-so-noble deeds is to help them rephrase their statements, beginning the sentence with "I . . . (followed by their action)." Next, we need to show them that their actions matter to others.

Key #2—Your Actions Affect Others

There is a golden rule in life that says to treat others the way you would like them to treat you. Every child needs to learn the Golden Rule early on because it sets the standard for learning how to treat others. It also communicates to the mind of a child that some things are good and some things are bad, and he or she should aspire to do what is good.

If I help my mother set the table, my mother feels happy. If I throw the football inside the house and break the lamp, my mother feels sad. If I say to my father, "I love you," my father feels loved. If I say to him, "I hate you," my father feels hurt. My words and my actions either help people or hurt people. When I help people, I feel good about myself. When I hurt people, I feel bad.

Life affords many opportunities to teach children that our actions affect others. When my (Arlene's) daughter Lucy was four, she hastily reached for a fork at the dinner table. She got the fork, but she also knocked over a bowl, which went crashing down on the tile floor. It shattered in so many pieces, pasta sauce everywhere. The bowl was a wedding gift. Out of the set of twelve, we had already broken at least half of the bowls.

In that instant, Lucy wondered, "Am I going to be in a lot of trouble?" I said, "It was an accident." My husband, James, went about getting the broom and the mop. Tears welled up in Lucy's eyes. I could tell she was sorry.

I instructed her, "Lucy, these plates are breakable, so you want to be extra careful with them. You didn't break it on purpose. It's okay. You can be more careful next time and when Daddy comes back in, you can apologize and thank him for cleaning up after the accident."

When James came back in to clean up, Lucy remained silent. Apologizing can be difficult! I prompted her. Her big brother and sister prompted her. When she finally opened her mouth, the apology came out in a gush of silly, bashful words. She didn't know what to say. I instructed her to look her daddy in the eyes as he was down on the floor cleaning up, and try again. Her second attempt was much better. Even though it was an accident, I wanted Lucy to apologize and connect the idea that what she does affects others.

Key #3—There Are Always Rules in Life

A third key in teaching children to apologize is helping them understand there are always rules in life. We've talked about the Golden Rule, which is most important, but there are many other rules designed to help us have a good life. "We don't throw the football inside the house" is a rule most parents have made for obvious reasons. Other rules include:

We don't take something that doesn't belong to us.
We don't tell things that are untrue about others.

We don't cross the street without looking both ways.
We say "thank you" when someone gives us something or says something nice about us.

When parents set rules for children, the overarching question should be: "Is this rule good for my child? Does it protect people or property?" Once parents have agreed on a rule, the entire family needs to be made aware of it. Unspoken rules are unfair rules. A child cannot be expected to live up to a standard of which she is unaware. Parents have the responsibility for making sure that children understand what the rules are. However, if you come to see that a particular rule is detrimental rather than helpful, then you should be willing to change that rule.

With the rules come consequences when the rules are broken. Consequences should be as closely associated with the rule as possible. For instance, if your child throws the football in the house, he loses the football for two days. It's ideal if the consequences for breaking family rules can be determined and discussed with the family at the time the rule is made. This gives the child the advantage of knowing ahead of time what the consequences will be if a rule is broken.

Parents are responsible for making sure the child receives the due consequences if an offense occurs. When parents are permissive one day and let misbehavior slide, and the next day come down hard on the child for the same misbehavior, the parents are on the sure road of rearing a disobedient, disrespectful child. Inconsistent discipline is the most common pitfall of parents who are trying to raise responsible children.

Few things are more important in teaching a child to apologize than establishing clear, meaningful rules. It develops a sense of morality: Some things are right, and some things are wrong.

When I do right, there are good results. When I do wrong, there are negative results. It is this sense of morality that helps the child understand the need for an apology.

Key #4—Apologies Will Restore Friendships

The fourth key in helping children learn to apologize is helping them understand that apologies are necessary in order to maintain good relationships. When I hurt other people by my words or my behavior, I have established a barrier between that person and me. My hurtful words or actions push people away from me, and without apology, they continue to walk away. The child, teenager, or adult who does not learn this reality will eventually end up isolated and alone.

With the help of his mother, Steven is learning this principle. He walked into the house one afternoon, flipped on the TV, and stretched out on the floor. "Why did you come in so early?" his mother, Sharon, asked. "You guys just started playing in the backyard."

"The other boys went home," he answered. "They didn't want to play the new game. I'm tired of playing the same old games. I told them that if they didn't want to play the new game, they could just go home."

The next afternoon when Sharon arrived home from work, she noticed that the neighborhood boys were not playing in the yard. Steven was again stretched out on the floor in front of the TV. "Are you guys not going to play this afternoon?" she asked. "The guys didn't show up," Steven said.

"Steven, I know you feel bad about this because I know how much you enjoy playing. I appreciate the fact that you like to try new games, but maybe what you said to the guys was too harsh."

"I didn't think they would really leave," Steven said. "I didn't even realize what I had said until they all walked away. I'm afraid now they're never going to come back and I don't have anybody to play with." Tears were forming in Steven's eyes.

Sharon's heart ached for her son. "I'm going to give you a suggestion, and I know it is going to be hard to do it. I think you need to apologize to your friends. Tell them you are sorry you got angry and told them to go home, that you have felt bad about it ever since, and ask them to forgive you."

"But, Mom, they'll think I am a wimp," he said.

"What they think is unimportant. What is important is what you know in your heart, and you know that you spoke those words in anger. I don't know whether they will forgive you. But I know that unless you apologize, they are not likely to come back. All of us get angry sometimes," she said, "and we sometimes say things that we later regret. But if we are willing to apologize, people will usually forgive us."

After dinner, Steven said, "I'm going to walk to the park, Mom, and see if the guys are there."

An hour later, Steven came in the house hot and sweaty. "How did it go?" Sharon asked.

"Cool. The guys were really cool. They said we all get mad sometimes and that it was okay. They asked me to play with them, and we had a good time. I told them we could play in our yard tomorrow."

"Great," his mother said. "Steven, I'm so proud of you. Those guys are fortunate to have a friend like you, and I'm fortunate to have a son like you."

The next afternoon, Sharon came home to find the neighborhood guys playing in the backyard. She breathed a sigh of relief and thanked God that it had gone well. Children must learn that friendships require honest apologies when we realize we have hurt our friends. The child who learns early that apologies restore friendships has learned one of the major lessons about human relationships.

Key #5—The Five Languages of Apology

The final key in teaching children how to apologize is to teach them how to speak the five languages of an apology:

Expressing Regret—"I am sorry."
Accepting Responsibility—"I was wrong."
Making Restitution—"What can I do to make it right?"
Genuinely Repenting—"I'll try not to do that again."
Requesting Forgiveness—"Will you please forgive me?"[1]

The level of proficiency should increase with age. It is very similar to the developmental process in learning to speak a language. A two-year-old can learn to say "I'm sorry" when she pulls the hair of her older sister. Or she could say, "I was wrong. I disobeyed," when she willfully does what she isn't supposed to. Thus, they are learning on the simplest level how to express regret and accept responsibility.

When the three-year-old pushes her brother down and he lies in a puddle of tears, the father may comfort the fallen soldier and teach the three-year-old to say, "I was wrong. I am sorry." And he might even encourage the offender to "go get a Band-Aid for your brother." With running for the Band-Aid, the child is learning to make restitution. Also at a very young age, children can learn to say, "I'll try not to do that again. Will you please forgive me?" and in so doing, they are learning the language of genuinely repenting and requesting forgiveness.

In early childhood (ages two through six), the child can learn to verbalize all five languages of an apology. During these early years, the motivation for apologizing is primarily external; that is, the parents are insisting that the child say "I'm sorry" or "I was wrong" or "I disobeyed." This is done in much the same way as we teach children to say "Thank you," "You're welcome," and "Please." The method is repetition, expectation, and sometimes, the withholding of privileges if the proper word is not spoken. The child learns primarily by outside prompting.

From grade one through grade twelve, the child learns to internalize these concepts and to speak these words from his or her own heart. A child may be able to text a parent or friend, "I was wrong. Please forgive me." That's a good start, but to fully experience that apology and forgiveness, it is best expressed in person. I (Gary) shall always remember the night my teenage son said to me, "I'm sorry, Dad. I was wrong. I should not have yelled at you. I hope that you will forgive me." Of course I did and shared with my wife the good news that apparently our hard work at trying to teach him to apologize was paying real dividends. I knew that if he could say those words to his father, then he would someday be able to say them to his wife and perhaps to his own children.

This leads me to observe that the most powerful method of teaching older children to speak the languages of apology is by your own model. When parents apologize to their children for harsh words or unfair treatment, they are doing their most effective teaching. Young children do what parents say; older children do what parents do.

The parent who reasons, "I don't want to apologize to my children because they will lose respect for me," is greatly deluded. The fact is the parent who sincerely apologizes to a child has just increased the child's respect for

The parent who reasons, "I don't want to apologize to my children because they will lose respect for me," is greatly deluded.

the parent. The child knows that what the parent did was wrong. The offense sits as a barrier between the parent and child. When the parent apologizes, the child is typically ready to forgive and the barrier is removed. Some of our finest moments are when we apologize to our children.

When children see adults apologizing to one another and to their kids, it helps them learn how to speak the languages of apology. To *speak* the apology—not to text or instant message or post on social media. If a child can practice saying "I'm sorry" in person, it will make a world of difference towards building healthy relationships in the future.

Things Not to Say When Apologizing to Your Kids

Do you want to use best practices for apologies that actually work? If so, omit these phrases when you are apologizing and teach them to do the same:

Haven't you gotten over that yet?
I should be excused because I...
Why do you always...?
If you hadn't...
That's just silly.
My bad.
That's life.
What's the big deal?
You're acting like a baby.
You just need to get over it.

Why can't you just forget about it?
You're too sensitive. I was only joking.
Your sister (or brother) would not have been upset by what I did.
Why can't you just leave it in the past?
You just need to be tougher.
I'm doing you a favor by apologizing.

Things to Say When Apologizing to Your Kids

Body language can make or break the sincerity of an apology. Be sure that you maintain eye contact, don't cross your arms defensively, listen with concern, and speak with a pleasant tone of voice. Then, choose words that do not blame others, excuse yourself, or deny responsibility.

I did it, and I have no excuse.
I'm responsible for the mistake.
I was careless.
I was insensitive.
I was rude.
My actions were not acceptable.
I will do the work to fix my mistake.
My heart aches over what I've done.

You didn't deserve that kind of treatment.
You have every right to be upset.
I know that what I did was wrong.
My mistake is part of a pattern that I need to change.
I will rebuild your trust by…
I will try to make this up to you by…
I've put you in a very difficult position.
I hope I haven't waited too long to say I am sorry.
Can you forgive me?

10

The A+ Skill of Attention

Pay attention; don't let life go by you.
Fall in love with the back of your cereal box.
—JERRY SEINFELD

How do you get kids to pay attention? That's a question psychologists Barbara Rogoff and Maricela Correa-Chavez wanted to answer. They ran a simple experiment, taking two kids into a room and sitting them at two tables. One child was taught how to assemble a toy. The other child was told to wait and in a few minutes, he or she would have a turn to make the toy.

What would your child do if told, "Wait"—pay attention, or mess around?

This experiment included two very different groups: middle-class kids from California and Mayan children from Guatemala. The results were crystal-clear. The Mayan kids were much more likely to pay attention, many of them sitting perfectly still, staring at the instructor. They showed sustained attention two-thirds of the time. In stark contrast, the majority of American kids zoned out and acted out, rarely paying attention at all.

Why the difference? Researchers concluded that Mayan kids are encouraged very young to pay attention to what their family is doing so they can learn how to do chores and work together as a unit. But there was another factor—an intrinsic *motivation* to pay attention. It turns out Mayan kids are much more autonomous (no helicopter parenting here) and used to making their own decisions over what they will and will not pay attention to. They aren't coerced or cajoled into paying attention; they *choose* to pay attention. Experts agree with the importance of this choosing. After studying kids and motivation for almost fifty years at the University of Rochester, psychologist Edward Deci says one of the most important ingredients for motivating kids is autonomy—"to do something with this full sense of willingness and choice."[1]

Like us, you've probably looked your child in the eyes and pleaded, "Now pay attention!" And usually that doesn't go so well. Ultimately, motivating your child to pay attention comes down to them understanding *why* they're doing something. Think about those Mayan children. How were they different from our kids? They weren't on screens. They were chasing baby chicks, doing chores with their mothers, climbing trees, and going to tech-free schools. Their *external environment* and *internal motivation* helped them to pay attention. Those two things can help your child pay attention too.

THE WANDERING MIND

Handing your child a screen might help pass the time on car rides, public transportation, and waiting at restaurants, but this convenient habit comes at a high cost. Children are becoming dependent on screens to function throughout the day. They rob autonomy from these future adults, because someday they will *need* the glow of a screen to accomplish just about anything. If you think this sounds overly dramatic, try taking away all screens from your child for just one day. Would you be able to notice a difference in them?

Children have the gift of curiosity. They naturally pay attention to the world around them, noticing many things that adults don't even see. But when a child is holding a phone, tablet, or controller, that natural ability to pay attention to the world disappears. Everything disappears except that bright rectangle. A little bit of screen time each day grows into a desire for more screen time. When your son isn't playing a video game, he's thinking about the next time he can play. When your daughter is in class, she's thinking about what she's going to post on social media later in the day. They may be physically present, but their minds are wandering.

Harvard PhD Matt Killingsworth studies the "wandering mind" and has collected over 650,000 real-time reports from more than 15,000 people from more than eighty countries. His big discovery? People's minds wander. A lot. Forty-seven percent of the time, people are thinking about something other than what they're currently doing. "This study shows that our mental lives are pervaded, to a remarkable degree, by the non-present," said Killingsworth.[2]

Researchers found that a wandering mind now is followed by unhappiness later. In other words, a wandering mind can steal happiness from both you and your child. When we fail to be fully present, we lose out on that moment of learning or connection with another human. What William James wrote in the late nineteenth century is relevant for today: "The faculty of voluntarily bringing back a wandering attention, over and over again, is the very root of judgment, character, and will."[3] Your child's ability to pay attention is not only an academic concern. It's a matter of happiness and the heart.

YOUR DIVIDED ATTENTION

I (Arlene) have a confession. Dear reader, while I am writing on my computer, my mind often drifts to "Hmm, I wonder if anyone has sent me a message?" "Let me check my email really fast." "Has my friend texted back?" When I can't fight the distraction any longer, I leave the pages of this manuscript for a rabbit trail of other endless things for me to click on. Sound familiar? Keeping focused on one task in the digital age is difficult for today's adult—and it's even harder for kids. Growing children especially need calm and quiet to develop those muscles of attention, focus, and deep thinking. Yet the screen world being offered does not promote any of those things.

Keeping focused on one task in the digital age is difficult for today's adult—and it's even harder for kids.

You're familiar with the term "information overload." Picture your child's mind as a cup. When your child spends too much time looking at screens, it's like constantly aiming a water hose at that cup. His mind is unable to retain and process the current of stimuli and information. To cope with all the information, he forms the habit of skimming all the information and going from one thing to the next. Tending to distractions becomes a way of life. One college freshman sent an email about how he has struggled with internet addiction since elementary school. "I can't focus on anything in school or at work in a deep or organized way. The only thing my mind wants to do is get back online and plug into games, news, and social media. I can't seem to concentrate on anything else."

But isn't it a modern marvel to multitask like a teenage ninja, doing homework, listening to your playlist, instant messaging, and watching a YouTube video at the same time? Actually no, because multitasking has its downsides—for kids and grown-ups. For starters, it reduces the quality of your work. In one experiment, students were asked to sit in a lab and complete a standard cognitive skill test. One group of subjects was not interrupted while taking the test. The other group was told they could be contacted with further instructions at any moment via text. They were interrupted twice during the exam. The interrupted group scored 20 percent less than the other group.[4] That difference is enough to bring a B-minus student down to an F for Failing student. In another study, researchers found that workers distracted by email and phone calls suffered a fall in IQ more than twice of that found in marijuana smokers.[5]

Multitasking also changes the way we learn. Research shows that people use different areas of the brain for learning and storing new information when they are multitasking. Brain scans of people who are distracted show activity in the striatum, a part of the brain used for learning new skills. Brain scans of people who are not distracted show activity in hippocampus, a region used for storing and recalling information.[6]

SCREEN TIME AND ATTENTION DISORDERS

If it seems like every kid you hear about has Attention Deficit Hyperactivity Disorder—you're not wrong. According to a national parent survey from 2016, 6.1 million children (9.4 percent) have been diagnosed with ADHD.[7] And the prevalence of screens is a factor.

In an Iowa State University study called "Television and Video Game Exposure and the Development of Attention Problems," 1,323 middle-childhood participants were observed over a thirteen-month period. Researchers found that six to twelve-year-olds who spent more than two hours a day playing video games or watching TV had trouble paying attention in school and were 1.6 to 2.1 times more likely to have attention problems. Dr. Dimitri Christakis, co-author of the study and associate professor of pediatrics at the University of Washington, says, "The concern is that the pacing of the program, whether it's video games or TV, is overstimulating and contributes to attention problems."[8] Another study of adolescents aged fifteen and sixteen, without symptoms of ADHD, found a significant association between higher frequency of digital media use and subsequent symptoms of ADHD when they followed up with the teens after two years.[9]

Clinical psychologist Dr. Catherine Steiner-Adair teaches extensively about technology and children. She says, "I have worked with children with ADD/ADHD and for many, proper medication makes all the difference in their ability to live up to their potential and thrive in school. But given the dramatic rise in the diagnosis of ADD/ADHD in recent years and growing concerns about the overmedication of children, we need to be more discerning. Given what we already know from research about the negative effects of media and screen play on children's self-regulation, attention, aggressive behaviors, sleep, and play patterns, we cannot ignore the possible link."[10]

Television shows, YouTube videos, and video games involve rapid changes of focus—compare the experience of watching an episode of Mister Rogers to watching *SpongeBob SquarePants*. Kids are trained to expect something to switch every few seconds. But real life doesn't work like that. Frequent exposure to ever-changing screens impacts a child's ability to sustain focus on tasks that aren't *designed* to be attention-grabbing. Experiencing constant excitement online makes it really hard for a child to downshift into, say, paying attention to a history lesson.

But isn't it good if my child can sit staring at a screen for hours? Not really, and that's because the reason they can pay continuous attention is because the screen content is giving them the pleasurable jolts of intermittent, unpredictable rewards. The attention a child brings to a video game is different from the concentration they need to succeed in regular life. A child can pay attention to a game fueled by frequent changes, constant rewards, new levels, points being racked up, and boosts of dopamine to the brain. When a child's brain grows accustomed to that fast pace, no wonder the real world becomes underwhelming and boring.

IN PRAISE OF READING

According to the Pew Research Center, eight out of ten parents say reading print books is very important for their children.[11] Reading is a foundational and multisensory experience for every child. She touches the page while her mind processes what she is reading. At times she must force herself to stay focused on the written words on the page. During reading time, things aren't changing every five seconds. You're following a storyline and engaging in a thought process. Children are learning how to stay with one topic and absorb something more deeply. Print reading, especially, strengthens her attention span muscles.

Nicholas Carr, in his landmark book *The Shallows: What the Internet Is Doing to Our Brains*, writes, "When we go online, we enter an environment that promotes cursory reading, hurried and distracted thinking, and superficial learning. It's possible to think deeply while surfing the Net, just as it's possible to think shallowly while reading a book, but that's not the type of thinking the technology encourages and rewards."[12]

Online reading is peppered with distracting hyperlinks and catchy headlines vying for your attention. In contrast, a book offers only one place to focus and therein offers great value for the growing child. Reading a book is a calming and relaxing activity. When a child puts down a book, he is usually in a good place. Contrast that to when a child puts down a tablet or phone. He is often argumentative ("Why can't I play longer?"), moody, and grumpy.

As a parent, you are able to guide your child's reading progress. For many kids, reading won't happen automatically. It must be scheduled in daily until it becomes an easy habit to maintain. Consider this comparison of three students with different reading habits.

Student A Reads	**Student B Reads**	**Student C Reads**
20 minutes per day	5 minutes per day	1 minute per day
3,600 minutes per school year	900 minutes per school year	180 minutes per school year
1,800,000 words per year	282,000 words per year	8,000 words per year
Scores in the 90th percentile on standardized tests	Scores in the 50th percentile on standardized tests	Scores in the 10th percentile on standardized tests

If they start reading for twenty minutes per night in kindergarten, by the end of sixth grade Student A will have read for the equivalent of sixty school days, Student B will have read for twelve school days, and Student C will have read for three.[13] Which student would you like your child to be?

ATTENTION BOOSTERS

Do you want your child to pay better attention in school and at home? One solution isn't found in educational software, more time hitting the books, or getting a tutor. According to the American Academy of Pediatrics, *play* is essential to cognitive development in children.[14] Playtime isn't video game time; it's time to throw a Frisbee, shoot a basketball, or play hopscotch.

Being outdoors is especially rejuvenating for the minds of children and adults alike. A series of psychological studies revealed that after spending time close to nature in a rural setting, people exhibited greater attentiveness, stronger memory, and generally improved cognition. Their brains were calmer and sharper.

Subjects were given a series of mentally fatiguing tests designed to measure their working memory and ability to exert control over their attention. After the test, one half of the group spent an hour walking through a secluded woodland park. The other half spent an hour walking along busy downtown streets. Both groups returned to take the test again. The group that spent the time in the park significantly improved their performance.[15]

The internet cannot provide the calming experiences that nature can. There are no puffy clouds for kids to look at or peaceful streams to skip a rock upon. A visit to your local park or preserve, or a day trip to a scenic place, will help your child calm his mind, preparing him to give the attention required at school and in life.

We've already discussed eye contact in terms of strengthening your relationship to your child, but teaching children to have eye contact with others also helps them to focus their attention on the person at hand. When you insist upon eye contact and give it generously, you are helping your child pay attention relationally to others and increasing their level of empathy.

Lastly, one of the biggest attention boosters is a good night's sleep. Sleep is an essential part of your child's healthy development. Studies have shown that kids who regularly get enough sleep have improved attention, behavior, learning, memory, and overall mental and physical health.[16]

The American Academy of Pediatrics recommends:[17]

Infants under 1 year: 12–16 hours
Children 1–2 years old: 11–14 hours
Children 3–5 years old: 10–13 hours
Children 6–12 years old: 9–12 hours
Teenagers 13–18 years old: 8–10 hours

A steady diet of screen time may hold your child's attention, but will it assist them in paying attention when it really counts? Both adults and children must learn how to pay attention to the important things of life. The rewards of this focused attention may not come immediately, but the payoff is long-lasting and life-changing.

Five Ways to Foster a Love of Reading in Your Child

1. Read aloud to your child. When your child is young, place them in your lap and read to them every day. Not only are you bonding with them and teaching them language, you are creating a happy memory that will draw them to books in the future. As your kids get older, they can sit next to you while you read a book the whole family will enjoy.

2. Visit the library regularly. Most things in life aren't free, but the library still is. Take advantage of the vast resources of your local library. Look up favorite authors in the library catalog and request those books if you don't see them immediately available. That will give your child something to look forward to during the next trip to the library. And don't forget to pick up a book for yourself.

3. Reading time for screen time. Some parents have successfully helped their children embrace books by making reading a prerequisite to screen time. If your child reads for thirty minutes, they can earn thirty minutes of screen time afterwards.

4. Find books that interest your child. What does your child enjoy? Whether stories about ponies or biographies of baseball heroes, look for books your child can't put down. Ask your friends with kids the same age or older for reading suggestions if you get stuck. Don't give up until you find a good fit for your reader.

5. Let them catch you reading. When your child sees you snuggled on the couch with a good book, it will encourage them to do the same. Talk to your kids about what you are reading and show them by your example that books are helpful and engaging.

Eight Ways to Help Your Child Finish Homework

1. Use games or charts for rewards. You can make a sticker chart where your child can place a sticker on each day that homework is done. Offer rewards for a completed week or month of homework. You can also create games to reward homework that is finished. For instance, if your child finishes homework all week, they can earn points. After fifty points, they can choose a small prize from the store.

2. Have a homework supply box. What does your child need to complete his homework—pencils, eraser, pens, ruler, stapler, glue, tape, and scissors? Have these supplies kept in one place so they are easy to find. If anything is taken out of the box, remember to replace it.

3. Know the best time for homework. Some kids like to start homework immediately after school so they can have the pleasure of free time afterward. Others need to run around for an hour after sitting at a desk for most of the day. Adjust your homework routine to what works best with your child.

4. Schedule out bigger projects. When your child comes home with a large or long-term project, create a calendar to help them break up the project into doable time chunks. Tell them a story about an assignment you procrastinated on to illustrate the value of doing a little bit at a time.

5. Work with a timer. If your child can complete their homework within half an hour, set a timer for thirty minutes and encourage them to finish before the timer beeps. If your child needs a longer time for homework, you can still set the timer for thirty minutes. When it beeps, take a five-minute break, and then resume the homework.

6. Offer healthy snacks. Children are often hungry after school. Avoid junk food, but instead offer healthy snacks like fruits or carrot sticks along with a glass of water.

7. Create an environment conducive to concentration. Is there enough light? Is the workspace uncluttered? Are the television and other electronic devices off? If your child needs to use the computer for homework, it is helpful if you can monitor usage to keep him on track.

8. Keep up the same schedule every week. Children thrive on predictable schedules. You may have to adjust your homework times on different days because you have sports practice on Tuesdays and Thursdays. As long as there is a consistent routine to follow that your child understands, they will be able to make those adjustments.

PART 3

Restart Your Home

11

Screen Time and You

I believe the most damaging effect of the digital world is the parent's own dependence on digital media because it will become their child's dependence.
—COLLEGE PASTOR

Russell, a father of three, works as an independent contractor and is constantly on his phone. There are jobs to check up on and future business to secure. Russell also volunteers at his church, heading up the men's ministry. He does a great job keeping men informed of upcoming events by calling and texting, but to his kids, Russell seems forever occupied with his phone.

Russell's wife, Nancy, isn't faring much better. Her kids and Russell's friends call her the "Twitter Queen," and that isn't meant as a compliment. Nancy scans through her tweets incessantly and posts several times a day. On date nights, she sits with Russell at dinner with phone in hand, replying to tweets and tweeting about her menu choices. Her constant connection to social media is driving Russell crazy, but he doesn't want to nag.

Russell and Nancy aren't the only parents having trouble balancing their screen time and family time. Parents are glued to their phones while they walk their kids from the parking lot to the schoolyard. At home, moms and dads constantly face screens, whether it's a computer, tablet, television, or phone. We're busy checking emails, social media, daily news, and text messages. Notifications grab our attention while our kids go unnoticed.

No child wants to compete with screens for their parents' attention, nor should they have to. Yet adults are becoming increasingly consumed with their devices, causing communication to erode with their children. Kids don't need constant attention from their parents, but they do need some undivided attention. Many children are frustrated, sad, and angry that they have to compete with screens for their parents' attention. Places that traditionally were spaces for a parent to connect with a child have become phone zones for many adults. A parent uses the phone in the car, during a park date, at birthday parties, and after dinner. It's socially acceptable behavior, but what does it communicate to your child? If a child constantly hears, "Hold on a minute, I'm on the phone," it communicates a message that spending time with your child is not nearly as important as what is happening on the phone.

I'M KIND OF HERE FOR YOU

Parents are more physically present in their children's lives than in generations past, but they are not necessarily emotionally present. Engagement between parents and children tends to be high-tech and low-quality. We may be just a few feet away from our kids, but we are constantly switching our attention between them and our devices, giving our kids what tech expert Linda Stone calls "continuous partial attention."[1]

In a survey of 6,000 children, researchers found that 54 percent of kids felt their parents checked their phone too often; 36 percent of kids said their parents' worst habit was getting distracted by their phones in the midst of conversation, and 32 percent said this made them feel unimportant.[2]

This bad habit has been called "technoference," a term coined by Brandon McDaniel, PhD, of Illinois State University.[3] Technoference refers to the interruptions in interpersonal communication caused by attention paid to devices instead. It is what's happening when you are looking at your phone and you don't hear the question your child asked you, even though you were supposedly listening. McDaniel and his team of researchers studied 170 families with children age five years or younger. They found parents who had a harder time managing their own phone use were more likely to experience technoference with their children, which was linked to worse behavior in the kids.

I (Arlene) was speaking to a pediatrician from Hawaii. He recalled a young, sleep-deprived couple bringing in their brand-new baby for an exam. The father sat in a chair next to mother and baby, physically present but mentally far away. He was playing video games on his phone. In that moment, the pediatrician decided to say something. "You have a responsibility to your wife and baby, so please put away your phone and learn how you can help."

"You have a responsibility to your wife and baby, so please put away your phone and learn how you can help."

Sometimes we need an outside voice to help us realize the static our technology use is creating in our most important relationships. We need to understand that the mere presence of a smartphone can undercut the quality of our interaction. In a study at the University of Chicago, researchers tested the "brain drain" hypothesis that just the presence of one's own smartphone occupies your limited cognitive resources. In other words, you are thinking about your nearby phone even though you're not touching it. You are ready to pick it up in a flash if it rings or vibrates. Researchers found that even when you exercise self-control and don't succumb to the temptation of picking it up, there is a brain cost.[4] Your brain isn't running on full capacity as you listen to your child. It is divided—and your child can sense that.

Please don't misunderstand this as a call for giving your kids your undivided attention all day long. That isn't reasonable or even healthy. It's beneficial for kids to be autonomous and play while a parent gets work done. Put your toddler in a playpen with toys without any guilt, then play with her later. Your child will be the better for it. But carve out time every day for your child to receive your full attention—with no devices competing.

NEVER UNPLUGGED

It doesn't matter if you're a stay-at-home parent or an ad executive. The temptation to constantly use screens is all around you. Technology addiction therapist Dr. David Greenfield says, "The phone's never off, so we're never off. . . . You sleep with it next to your pillow. We're not designed to be vigilant 24-7."[5]

The wired world has moved the workplace right into the family living room. We are no longer forced to leave our work behind at an office desk; we take endless emails and problems home with us through our devices. Employers capitalize on this connectivity by expecting emails and texts to be responded to immediately, even after hours. Is it really that important to be plugged in 24/7 to your work? For some professions, the answer is yes. But for most, the answer is no.

For many parents, it's not really a job that is keeping them tied to a phone all day. It's simply become a habit to be constantly checking the phone, scrolling through emails, or clicking through channels. Friends and family have come to expect instant responses to texts. Yet the smartphone was created to make your life more convenient. If you don't answer the phone, the caller can leave a voicemail or choose to text. You don't have to reply right away. The information isn't going anywhere. If you take a call or answer a text while you are talking to your children, you're setting a model for them. The phone takes precedence over talking with one another.

Of course there will be exceptions when you are anticipating an important call and you tell your family members you will need to take it whenever it comes. If you are in the middle of texting and your child wants to talk to you, it's fine to say, "Honey, let me finish this text." After finishing the text, give her your undivided attention, face-to-face, for those few seconds as she asks a question or makes a comment. That short, focused, positive interaction communicates, "You are important to me."

Cellphones by the Numbers

According to the Pew Research Center:

96% of American adults have a cellphone[6]

81% of American adults have a smartphone[7]

28% of American adults go online "almost constantly"[8]

33% of American adults use their phone to watch movies or TV[9]

46% say when using the Internet, they mostly use their phone[10]

46% describe their smartphone as something they "couldn't live without"[11]

GROWING UP JUST LIKE YOU

Children learn from imitating parents from the very start. Professors Andrew Meltzoff and Patricia Kuhl from the University of Washington show videos of babies at forty-two minutes old imitating adults. When the adult stuck his tongue out, the baby did the same. Not even one hour old, and the babies mirrored the adults' behavior.[12] When you became a parent, you quickly realized that a little baby was counting on you for protection and direction. Now that your baby has grown into a child, he needs you to be digitally wise because chances are he is going to grow up to imitate your example.

Young children watch where a parent focuses attention and will follow a mother's gaze. When parents exhibit a fascination with phones, tablets, or computers, children naturally will be curious about those things too. If the phone is the central focus of a parent's attention, a toddler is going to think, "I need to play with *that*!"

What we *model* digitally is more important than what we *say* about screen time. If we as parents are totally consumed all of our waking hours with electronic media of any kind, we are communicating, *"This is what life is about. This is the norm."* Too often parents give the right message but in the wrong manner. We tell our children to limit screen time, but then we spend hours online after work. We say social media is unhealthy but we've got it up throughout the day. We say video games are a waste of time, and then spend two hours after work unwinding with a game. As one child said, "My parents say that I waste a lot of time with my iPad, but I see them doing exactly the same thing."

It seems unfair to a child when he is expected to do something that his parent hasn't even been able to do. As the late Howard Hendricks said so well, "You cannot impart what you do not possess."[13] The most effective teaching takes place when a parent shows a child how to manage the digital world wisely out of her own positive experience with technology. If your digital role model isn't quite ready to be imitated by your children, it may be time for you to take a break yourself and launch a digital reset. For more help with this, we recommend Arlene's book *Calm, Cool, and Connected: 5 Digital Habits for a More Balanced Life.*

DIGITAL SABBATH AND SPACES

When my (Arlene's) husband and I were married more than twenty years ago, he had a strange request. Could we have a TV-free home for the first month of our marriage? He wanted to spend quality time together in the evenings after work instead of turning on the tube. Although it was quite a stretch (I was working as a television producer then), we did it. When we brought the television back, it seemed like a noisy intruder to our peaceful oasis. We've never subscribed to cable since.

As a result, our children aren't up on the latest programs. They've never had the television on as background noise. When it is movie night or we watch a funny video online, it's an event and the kids come running. But I can honestly say a media-poor life has given us a family-rich life. Ethan, Noelle, and Lucy have grown up with a love of books, music, exercise, biking, and plenty of time for imaginative play. Now I am not advocating that canceling cable or streaming services is for every household. But I do want to encourage you that it is possible to raise your children differently even in a media-saturated world.

Now before you think I'm unaffected by screen time, let me confess. I may not watch TV, but my home computer is always humming. I'm constantly sitting in front of my computer, writing books, recording videos, checking emails and social media, and updating my calendar. My kids know I'm an author who works from home, which legitimizes my screen time. But I know many times I'm shopping on Amazon or watching a YouTube video, spending unnecessary minutes with my screens instead of taking a break.

Spouses are especially gifted at pointing out areas of improvement and when I asked James about my screen time, he exclaimed, "You are *always* on your computer!" As a result of this realization, I am doing an experiment by turning off my computer after dinner. This forces me to be more productive in the day time and ensures that I won't waste my time mindlessly online in the evening.

When you set a curfew for all your gadgets and power off at the same time each night, it will actually prepare you to have a better night's rest. You can put yourself, not just your kids, on a schedule. How much television are *you* going to watch per day? How long are *you* going to stay online?

William Powers, author of *Hamlet's Blackberry: A Practical Philosophy for Building a Good Life in the Digital Age*, decided to try a simple experiment to bring back the notion of a refreshing weekend. He and his family created their own digital Sabbath by unplugging their home modem from Friday at bedtime until Monday morning. At first, it was incredibly hard for Powers, his wife, and their son. They saw how badly they needed digital connection when they saw how hooked they were. After two months of dark computer screens on weekends, it started to get easier, and after four or five months, they began to actually enjoy the benefits. Notice things didn't change overnight:

> *We'd peeled our minds away from the screens where they'd been stuck. We were really there with one another and nobody else, and we could all feel it. . . . There was an atmospheric change in our minds, a shift to a slower, less restless, more relaxed way of thinking. We could just be in one place, doing one particular thing, and enjoy it . . . The digital medium allows everything to be stored for later use. It was still out there, it was just a little further away. The notion that we could put the crowd, and the crowded part of our life, at a distance like this was empowering in a subtle but significant way. It was a reminder that it was ours to put at a distance.*[14]

I (Gary) posted a question on my Facebook page about how to create more distance between us and our digital devices. Here are a few of the responses:

We are putting a bin at our front door with a sign that says, "Unless you are expecting a call from God, the Pope, or the President—please deposit your device here so we can make the most of our time together.

We unplug from the time we get home until we get up again the next morning.

Wireless is on a timer so it goes off at night.

Dinnertime is always screen-free time.

There are many ways you can tailor-make a digital Sabbath that will work well for you and your family. As you pull away from the noise of the screen, you will be able to tune into the hearts of your children more easily.

PARENTAL CONTROLS FOR PARENTS

In an advice column in the *Wall Street Journal,* one parent asked:

Dear Dan,

I waste about two hours each day playing stupid games on my iPhone. It feels so innocent, but it actually makes me lose focus at work and takes up time I should be spending with my wife and kids. Do you have an idea for how I can ditch this bad habit?

Here is the answer from columnist Dan Ariely:

> *One way to fight bad habits is to create rules. When you start a diet, for example, you can set yourself a rule such as "I won't drink sugary beverages." But to be effective, rules need to be clear and well defined . . . In your case, you could decide that, from now on you won't be playing on the iPhone between 6 a.m. and 9 p.m. And to help you follow this rule, you should let your loved ones know. Or you could set up game bans for weekdays or working hours. Good luck.*[15]

Digital rules aren't only good for kids; they are great for parents too. Be specific when you create rules about time limits, content allowed, and what you make exceptions for. We understand it's not easy to implement new rules. In fact, since so many adults can't curb their online use alone, there are programs that track, report, and limit digital activity, such as Apple's Screen Time. Accountability to a spouse or friend is also effective when both parties know what to ask and report, and establish rewards and consequences.

Use positive language when you are creating new digital house rules for yourself. Don't put the emphasis on *disconnecting,* as if you are losing out. Instead focus on *connecting* and what you will be gaining through spending more time with your kids. Cal Newport, author of *Digital Minimalism,* encourages us to establish a digital philosophy. What do you want technology to do for your kids and for your family? Keep to those values and avoid using tech when it doesn't serve those values. Focus your online time on a small number of carefully selected activities that support your principles, and happily miss out on everything else.[15]

Jody, mother of four, noticed that she needed to change the screen time rules around her house, not only for her kids but for her. She decided to try a "digital detox" for a few days and made these observations:

> *Even just after one day, the kids were calmer and more apt to have a more thoughtful conversation with each other. The urge for Minecraft, My Little Pony, YouTube, Google, etc., was taking over their ability to be empathetic with one another. In all honesty, I found myself battling it too. I almost want to chuck my phone out the window because I'll check email, then find myself on Facebook or Instagram. It just makes me so inattentive and unproductive, which is completely opposite of what it's supposed to do. I don't want my kids to remember me as unfocused.*

What digital guidelines would help you personally make the most out of your screen time? Sabbath days when you take a break from screens? A cutoff time in the evening? A bin to place your phone during mealtimes? Every person is different, so cater your plan to fit your family's schedule and priorities. But do set specific guidelines or else you risk wasting many precious hours online when you could be creating permanent bonds with your spouse or children.

SAYING GOODBYE TO THE ELECTRONIC BABYSITTER

Finally, you may be ready to make personal screen time changes, but you aren't ready to give up the electronic babysitter for your children. Neil, father of two boys ages two and four, relies on the television to entertain the boys after he gets home from work. His wife works in the evenings and he needs some time to unwind from a busy day and to make dinner. "When the boys are in front of the television, they are quiet and calm. I must confess it's a great babysitter when you need one."

It's certainly easier to allow your children to watch hours of television than to provide alternative activities or monitor their behavior. But the easy way is not always the best way. What results can an electronic babysitter yield compared to an involved, proactive parent? What you do in the first eighteen years of your child's life is monumental in their development into adults. Your investment as a parent will pay huge dividends in your child's life, particularly in the young adult years.

We are sympathetic to the parents who are getting by and taking the path of least resistance out of desperation. But as a parent, you've got to purpose in your heart to fight against the negative effects of screen time and electronic babysitters. Begin with an honest inspection of how you use screen time in your own life and with your children. You hold in your hand a golden opportunity to teach your child how to master their screen time—by learning to master your own.

12

Top Ten Questions and Answers

▶ **I have a middle schooler, but I'm not sure he is ready for a phone. How can you tell?**

Here are a few life skills your child should have mastered (without complaining or nagging) to demonstrate he or she is ready for a phone:

Make school lunch everyday
Do laundry completely and contribute with household chores
Complete homework and do well in school
Get up with alarm
Wash the car
Cook a full meal
Manage money
Is able to carry on a conversation with adults
Personal hygiene
Take care of pets[1]

If your child is not responsible with tasks like these, it is unreasonable to think he or she will be responsible with a phone.

You have to consider the capability of the device you're considering and the emotional development of your child. What purpose would the device serve your child at this age?

When in doubt, delay. We suggest starting with a basic phone, not a smartphone. As one father said, "Taking away a smartphone is much harder than just not giving one at all."

▶ Arlene, your high schooler doesn't have a phone. How does he manage that with school and staying in touch with friends?

Don't let anyone make you think your child can't survive academically or socially without a phone. Ethan enjoys good grades in all his AP and Honors classes. He has a free Google voice account, so he can text and call friends from the computer. He's welcome to use my phone at home to call or text friends. He borrows his friend's phone when he has to text me to coordinate getting picked up. He rides his bike to school so he is very independent. When he's gotten a flat tire (with no phone), he just walks home like in the "good old days." Ethan is involved in after-school activities and church, and has healthy friendships with other kids and adults. It's important that your child has non-screen interests, so being "phone deprived" doesn't ruin one's life. Activities for Ethan we've invested in (instead of phone) include martial arts, piano lessons, mountain biking, skiing, and camping.

▶ What can I do if it's my husband who plays video games with the kids all weekend?

First you can start with the positive. Your husband is spending time with the children. Many kids don't have a dad to play with. Let's affirm your husband first for spending time with the kids instead of being critical, and maybe praise him more than once for this. Then, you can say something like this later, "I wonder if instead of playing video games this time, if you can take Johnny to the backyard and play ball with him. He's been talking about football and I'm sure he'd love for you to teach him how to catch. I'm concerned that he might think the only thing you do together is play video games, and I want him to have other memories with you besides video games."

Since you've been affirming your husband, he's far more likely to take your suggestion to heart. If you come to him with a request, rather than a demand, he will be much more open to your idea. If you just come in with a critical attitude and say things like "I just read video games are awful for the kids," or "Can't you do something else besides those video games?" he may just think "Get off my back!" He will most likely get defensive and just return to more video game playing with the kids.

▶ What if my son is left out because his friends all play video games?

Perhaps, like many parents, you fear that video games are the main way boys connect with each other. The problem is we underestimate the addictive nature of video games and the risks—as we have seen. Melanie Hempe, BSN, says that boys have different developmental needs at different ages.[2] For example, thirteen-year-olds are usually socially awkward. During this season when they need to develop real social skills, they can retreat to gaming, which is a low-effort, high-reward activity. It's challenging to be social in person but it's easy to play games and pretend that games are social. Older gamer boys get stuck in this stage: they can play alongside other boys through gaming, but they may not possess adequate face-to-face skills, leadership, empathy, or communication skills.

When we understand these risks, it's easier to see the problem of being like everyone else. Your son can look for friends who aren't gamers. In the short term, it may feel like he doesn't have as many friends, but in the long term, he will have a much easier time making friends in the future. Often boys have no idea who they are playing games with. They sit for hours in one place, spending less and less time in the real world. Gamers can be very limited in their conversational skills unless they are talking with other gamers. As an adult, these limitations will make your son feel left out in the workplace, college, and someday a family. Better to be left out of gaming now, but not left out in life later on.

▶ What if me and my spouse disagree about how much screen time is right for the kids?

Any time you have a disagreement on any topic, there are three possible ways to resolve it after you've both talked about it and had a chance to explain your reasoning.

I'll meet you on your side. Picture a straight line with an X on each end, representing the husband and the wife. This means that one of you actually goes all the way to the other side and basically says, "After I've listened to your reasoning, I think I'll go with your perspective."

Meet you in the middle. You come to a compromise. If your spouse thinks six hours of screen time is fine, but you want only two hours, you settle on four hours of screen time.

Meet you later. This is when it's pretty obvious that you are not going to agree in one sitting. You agree to disagree for the moment, get a good night's sleep, and pick it up again the following week. You agree to disagree instead of preaching a sermon and ending the evening angry.

Perhaps one of you thinks your daughter is ready for a phone at age ten, but the other parent thinks fourteen would be a better age. Ask your spouse, "Why do you think she's ready at ten?" and really listen and try to understand the other person's perspective. You might come to a middle ground and land on age twelve, deciding to evaluate the situation again when your daughter is twelve. You are constantly fishing for one of these three solutions, no matter what the topic of conflict.

▶ What if Grandma buys a phone but we do not want it?

Begin by giving Grandma the benefit of the doubt. She had good intentions and thought she was buying something your child would really like. You can talk with your child and say something like, "That was very considerate of Grandma to buy you a phone. We are going to have specific guidelines for how you can use it." You may want to limit the phone to be used only at home to call Grandma. If you feel your child is not ready for a phone, however, you may respectfully talk to Grandma and share a few of the reasons you believe the phone will be a detriment. You may want to recommend our book *Grandparenting Screen Kids*. You can share what you've learned about the impact of too many screens on a child's brain. She may want to return it and save it for a later time.

If your child is in middle school or older, you can establish rules before leaving the phone with your child. These rules might be things like charging the phone overnight outside of the bedroom and a limit of fifteen minutes per day after school.

▶ I'm concerned with how much screen time is in school now. What can we do?

If you have a concern, other parents probably do too. If your administrators hear from several parents, they are more likely to act. My (Arlene) husband James is on the parent board at our public elementary school and he was able to voice his concerns about phones on campus. The administrators were also concerned, so the kids are not allowed to have phones out during the school day. Recess has been saved; kids aren't staring down at the phones anymore.

We have bought the idea that technology will make our kids more productive and smarter in the classroom, but there is not research to back that up. A global education study found that "there is no single country in which the internet is used frequently at school by a majority of students and where students' performance improved."[3]

There may be value in a class looking at a website together and talking about it. However, young people are accustomed to using their devices for entertainment purposes, not educational ones.

In a pro-educational technology training video, a teenager says, "I'm not posting selfies to Instagram. I'm actually in a Google Hangout typing questions to researchers in Botswana about water conservation methods." The training video makes it appear easy for teens to use technology constructively. Matt Miles is a high school teacher, and when he shows this video with his students, they laugh. One student said, "If you see me on my phone, there's a zero percent chance I'm doing something productive. If you see me on my laptop, there's a 50 percent chance." Most students thought 50 percent was too high. In reality, students use computers to play games, post selfies, message parents and friends, and watch videos. Matt, who has also coauthored *Screen Schooled: Two Veteran Teachers Expose How Technology Use is Making Our Kids Dumber,* says, "When teachers put devices in the hands of kids and expect them to be productive, they're expecting too much. Teaching kids with technology is analogous to having an AA meeting in a bar."[4]

▶ Is there a difference in learning between reading a physical book and reading on a tablet?

There is a valuable physicality in reading a book with actual pages. You're looking at left and right pages and can often picture where you read a certain sentence or passage to find it in the future. You can easily tell how far along you are in the book to give you a sense of place. You can fold a page that interests you and highlight the text easily. In contrast, a reader of digital text might scroll through a stream of words, tapping forward one page at a time. Once the page is read, it's gone.

In one university study, tenth-grade students of similar reading ability studied one narrative and one expository text of about 1,500 words each. Half the students read on paper and half of them read on PDF files on computers with fifteen-inch LCD monitors. Students who read on the computers scored worse than the ones who read on paper. The students on the computer could only scroll or click through sections of the PDF, but students reading on paper could hold the text in its entirety and switch between pages. The researchers concluded that paper may be better suited for reading comprehension.[5]

Also, when reading a physical book, there is only one thing for your child to do. But when your child holds an e-reader, he or she has to spend mental energy to fight the temptation to browse other books or click on related links. People don't usually bring as much mental effort to screens in the first place. Your child might read happily in a corner for a half hour, but when reading online, after a few minutes, she gets bored and starts clicking on other things.

▶ I monitor what's on my child's device, but I don't know what his friends are showing him. What can I do when my child is at a friend's house or at school?

You can't impose your rules on another family or your child's friends. But you can certainly have helpful conversations to keep pornography, bullying, and inappropriate images and comments from harming your child. Here are a few guidelines you can use when making decisions about screen times and friends:

Differentiate the big things from the small things. Ask yourself, "Will this matter a week from now?" If your child is viewing porn at someone's house, the answer will be yes. But if he is occasionally playing thirty minutes of non-violent video games, the answer is probably no.

Get to know your child's friends. Take the time to befriend the parents of your children's friends. You need to be able to ask, "What types of television shows and video games do you allow in your home? Do you know what the girls are watching?" Don't think it is rude to ask; it is your responsibility as a parent to create safe boundaries for your child even when she is away from you.

Make yourself the fall guy. You might fear appearing judgmental and superior if you ask too many questions. Just tell the other parent that you are overprotective. It's more gracious to criticize yourself ("Forgive me if I'm such a high-maintenance parent") than to implicate the more lenient parent.

If you find your family's screen time values are not compatible with the other family, it's probably a good idea to distance yourself from that friend after school. Every family has the right to have different values. It's not a case of your son being too good for another boy. It's a matter of you as a parent being the protector of your child.

Teach your child to look away. Tell your children if a person shows them something they are not comfortable with to look away. You can choose where your eyes go. Turning away from lewd, inappropriate, mean, or sexual images will help your child mature as he learns to guard his heart from evil.

CLOSING THOUGHTS

The good news is that it's never too late to start doing what's healthy. It's true on the individual level and it's true in our parenting. Any life can be turned around. As long as your children are living in your house, it's not too late to become more actively involved in teaching and training your children in things you think are healthy.

Approach your child like a coach (not a friend). Be warm, excited, and confident when you share the new habits you will be practicing in your family. Your younger kids might be wide-eyed with excitement over doing crafts instead of video games if you are excited about it! With your older kids, you might say something like this: "We have not done a very good job in the area of screen time and video games. We haven't been paying attention to what you have been playing. We deeply regret this. We have let you down in this area. But we're going to change things. We are going to guide you from now on. Will you forgive us for being absent when we should have been here to help you?"

Owning up for your responsibility as a parent is much more effective than accusing your child of poor decision-making. As you decide what's healthy for your family and articulate a clear media game plan moving forward, your family will thrive within the boundaries you set. Here are a few action steps you might implement as a result of reading *Screen Kids*:

- No screens present during mealtimes.
- Delay smartphones and social media until high school.
- Cancel one streaming service.
- Complete a four-to-six-week electronic reset with no devices.
- No screens allowed in the bedroom.
- Reduce or eliminate video games.

When my (Gary's) children were growing up, we set a guideline of no more than thirty minutes a day of television. That was a long time ago and screens weren't nearly as prevalent in the home. But setting that time limit for television was critical because my children could have watched hours every day if my wife, Karolyn, and I didn't have a plan. The same principles that guided our home decades ago still hold true today. The close-knit family of yesteryear can be your reality in this present digital age.

When you have a purpose and a plan, technology can be a tool to bring your family closer together. But left as a default activity, technology as a toy will rob your family of quality time and memories together every time. So what kind of home will you create for your family? A home that is centered around screens or a home that is centered around people? When you have the latter, you will be drastically different from the average tech-driven home. Your home will be like a castle on a hill, providing light not only to your children, but to your world.

Quiz: Does Your Child Have Too Much Screen Time?

These simple questions can help determine whether or not screen time is harming your child's overall health. Give a score to each question using the following ratings:

0 = Never or rarely true
1 = Occasionally true
2 = Usually true
3 = Always true

_____ Your child is upset when you ask him to stop his screen activity to come to dinner or another activity.

_____ Your child asks you to buy a digital device such as an iPad after you have already said no.

_____ Your child has trouble completing his homework because he is busy watching television or playing video games.

_____ Your child refuses to help with chores around the house, choosing instead to play with screens.

_____ Your child asks you if he can play a video game or other screen related activity after you have said no.

_____ Your child does not get 60 minutes of physical activity each day.

_____ Your child does not give frequent eye contact to others in the home.

_____ Your child would rather play video games than go outside to play with friends.

_____ Your child doesn't really enjoy anything that does not involve screens.

_____ If you restricted all screen use for one day, your child would be irritable and whiny.

If your child scores:

10 or below: Your child does not appear to have too much screen time. He seems able to exercise appropriate control and boundaries.

11–20: Your child may be depending on screen time too much. You will want to monitor screen time more judiciously and watch for growing reliance upon screens.

21–30: Your child may be addicted to screens. You may want to meet with a counselor, pastor, or parent that you respect for advice.

Quiz: Is Your Child Addicted to Video Games?

0 = No

1 = Sometimes

2 = Yes

_____ During the past year, has your child become more preoccupied with playing video games, studying video game playing, or planning the next opportunity to play?

_____ Does your child need to spend more time and/or money on video games than he or she used to?

_____ Does your child become restless or irritable when told to cut back or stop playing video games?

_____ Does your child play video games to escape problems, bad feelings, or homework?

_____ Has your child lied about how much they play video games or about anything related to gaming?

_____ Does your child neglect household chores to spend more time playing video games?

_____ Has your child done poorly on a quiz, test, or homework because he or she was gaming instead of studying?

_____ Does your child want to play video games every single day?

_____ Does your child say he or she is bored unless gaming?

_____ Has your child skipped sports or other hobbies to get more game time?

_____ Does your child play games after you are in bed at night?

_____ Does your child get depressed if he or she isn't allowed to play?

_____ Do you have a gut feeling your child is addicted to video games?

_____ Has your child tried and failed to quit or reduce video game playing?

_____ Do you have conflict over video gaming in your home?

If your child scores:

8 or below: Your child appears to be a casual gamer. He or she likes video games but enjoys other activities more.

9–15: Your child is becoming more and more engrossed in gaming. He or she is at risk of becoming dependent on gaming.

15–30: Your child has a problem with video gaming. It's time to make changes so he or she will not succumb to video game addiction.[1]

Notes

Authors' Note

1. Adolescent Brain Cognitive Development Study, accessed March 9, 2020, https://abcdstudy.org.
2. World Health Organization, "Coming of Age: Adolescent Health," accessed September 2, 2019, https://www.who.int/health-topics/adolescents/coming-of-age-adolescent-health.
3. "The Common Sense Census: Media Use by Kids Age Zero to Eight," Common Sense Media, 2017, https://www.commonsensemedia.org/sites/default/files/uploads/research/0-8_executivesummary_release_final_1.pdf, 3.
4. Jessica Stillman, "Severely Limited Their Kids' Tech Use," *Inc.*, October 29, 2017, https://www.inc.com/jessica-stillman/why-steve-jobs-bill-gates-both-severely-limited-their-kids-tech-use.html.
5. Chris Anderson, "My 12 Rules for Kids and Screens," Medium, October 27, 2018, https://medium.com/@chr1sa/my-12-rules-forkids-and-screens-d7e46390589b.
6. Kristin Weir, "A Deep Dive into Adolescent Development," American Psychological Association, *Monitor on Psychology* 50, no. 6 (June 2019), https://www.apa.org/monitor/2019/06/adolescent-development.

Introduction

Epigraph: Kimberly Young, quoted in Adam Alter, *Irresistible: The Rise of Addictive Technology and the Business of Keeping Us Hooked* (New York: Penguin Books, 2017), 166.

1. "The Common Sense Census: Media Use by Kids Age Zero to Eight," Common Sense Media, 2017, https://www.commonsensemedia.org/sites/default/files/uploads/research/0-8_executivesummary_release_final_1.pdf, 3.
2. "Media Use by Tweens and Teens 2019: Infographic," Common Sense Media, October 28, 2019, https://www.commonsensemedia.org/Media-use-by-tweens-and-teens-2019-infographic, 3.
3. Andy Crouch, *The Tech-Wise Family: Everyday Steps for Putting Technology in Its Proper Place* (Grand Rapids: Baker Books, 2017), 23.

4. "Screen Time and Children," MedlinePlus, accessed October 2, 2019, https://medlineplus.gov/ency/patientinstructions/000355.htm.
5. Jacqueline Howard, "Kids Under 9 Spend More Than 2 Hours a Day on Screens, Report Shows," *CNN Health*, October 19, 2017, https://www.cnn.com/2017/10/19/health/children-smartphone-tablet-use-report/index.html.
6. Alter, *Irresistible*, 3.
7. Ibid., 208.
8. Adam Alter, "How Technology Gets Us Hooked," *Guardian*, February 28, 2017, https://www.theguardian.com/technology/2017/feb/28/how-technology-gets-us-hooked.
9. Alter, *Irresistible*, 162.
10. The Common Sense Census: Media Use by Kids Age Zero to Eight," Common Sense Media, 2017, https://www.commonsensemedia.org/sites/default/files/uploads/research/0-8_executivesummary_release_final_1.pdf, 15.
11. "Social Media, Social Life: Teens Reveal Their Experiences," Common Sense Media, September 10, 2018, https://www.commonsensemedia.org/social-media-social-life-infographic, 18.
12. Drake Baer, "Malcolm Gladwell Explains What Everyone Gets Wrong about His Famous '10,000 Hour Rule,'" Business Insider, June 2, 2014, https://www.businessinsider.com/malcolm-gladwell-explains-the-10000-hour-rule-2014-6.
13. Crouch, *The Tech-Wise Family*, 128.
14. "The Common Sense Census," Common Sense Media, 17.

Chapter 1: Screen Time and the Brain

Epigraph: Nicholas Kardaras, *Glow Kids: How Screen Addiction Is Hijacking Our Kids and How to Break the Trance* (New York: St. Martin's Griffin, 2016), 14.

1. Andrew Perrin, "5 Facts about Americans and Video Games," Pew Research Center, September 17, 2018, https://www.pewresearch.org/fact-tank/2018/09/17/5-facts-about-americans-and-video-games/.
2. Shawn Radcliffe, "Is Screen Time Altering the Brains of Children?," Healthline, December 19, 2018, https://www.healthline.com/health-

news/how-does-screen-time-affect-kids-brains#Questions-about-screen-timeremain.
3. "Victoria Dunckley MD," ScreenStrong, YouTube, November 8, 2018, https://www.youtube.com/watch?v=SWQuNnCdN5Y.
4. "The Drug-Like Effect of Screen Time on the Teenage Brain," PBS NewsHour, May 4, 2016, https://www.pbs.org/newshour/show/the-drug-like-effect-of-screen-time-on-the-teenage-brain.
5. Tanya Basu, "Just How Bad is Kids' Smartphone Addiction?," Stanford University, January 9, 2018, https://neuroscience.stanford.edu/news/just-how-bad-kids-smartphone-addiction.
6. Joanna Stern, "Disney+, Apple TV+ and More: How to Watch TV in This Confusing Age," *Wall Street Journal*, November 9, 2019, https://www.wsj.com/articles/disney-apple-tv-and-more-how-to-watch-tv-in-this-confusing-age-11573272000?mod=searchresults&page=1&pos=8.
7. The Brain Warrior's Way Podcast, "The Difference Between Pleasure and Happiness with Dr. Robert Lustig," September 19, 2019, https://brainwarriorswaypodcast.com/the-difference-between-pleasure-happiness-with-dr-robert-lustig/.
8. "The Best Natural Ways to Increase Serotonin," BrainMD, January 20, 2019, https://brainmd.com/blog/4-ways-to-boost-your-serotonin/.
9. University of Maryland, College Park, "Students around the World Report Being Addicted to Media, Study Finds," ScienceDaily, April 5, 2011, www.sciencedaily.com/releases/2011/04/110405132459.htm.
10. Joe Clement and Matt Miles, *Screen Schooled: Two Veteran Teachers Expose How Technology Use Is Making Our Kids Dumber* (Chicago: Chicago Review Press, 2018), 39.
11. "Internet Gaming," American Psychiatric Association, https://www.psychiatry.org/patients-families/internet-gaming.
12. "FAQs," NetAddiction, http://netaddiction.com/faqs/.
13. "S Korean dies after games session," BBC, August 10, 2005, http://news.bbc.co.uk/2/hi/technology/4137782.stm.
14. "The Spectrum of Video Gaming Activity: From Casual Use to Addiction," comp. Victory Dunckley and Malanie Hempe, Screen Strong, accessed June 15, 2020, https://screenstrong.com/video-games/additionalresources/.
15. Melanie Hempe, *Will Your Gamer Survive College*? (Charlotte, NC: Families Managing Media, 2018), 10.

16. "TEDxRainier - Dimitri Christakis - Media and Children," TEDx Talks, YouTube video, December 28, 2011, https://www.youtube.com/watch?v=BoT7qH_uVNo.
17. Kurt W. Fischer, William T. Greenough, Daniel Siegel, and Paul Thompson, "How Much Do We Really Know about the Brain?," *Frontline*, 2002, http://www.pbs.org/wgbh/pages/frontline/shows/teenbrain/work/how.html.
18. "Interview: Jay Giedd," *Frontline*, 2002, https://www.pbs.org/wgbh/pages/frontline/shows/teenbrain/interviews/giedd.html.
19. Nicholas Carr, *The Shallows: What the Internet Is Doing to Our Brains* (New York: W. W. Norton & Company, 2011), 121.
20. Ibid., 77.
21. Clement and Miles, *Screen Schooled*, 23.
22. Robin Marantz Henig, "Scientist at Work: Benjamin S. Carson; For Many, Pediatric Neurosurgeon Is a Folk Hero," *New York Times*, June 8, 1993, https://www.nytimes.com/1993/06/08/science/scientist-work-benjamin-s-carson-for-many-pediatric-neurosurgeon-folk-hero.html.

Chapter 2: Screen Time and Relationships

Epigraph: Andy Stanley, *Five Things God Uses to Grow Your Faith Participant's Guide* (Grand Rapids: Zondervan, 2009), 35.

1. "Social Media, Social Life: Teens Reveal Their Experiences, 2018," Common Sense Media, https://www.commonsensemedia.org/research/social-media-social-life-2018, 8.
2. Doree Lewak, "Video Game Addiction Ruined My Life," *New York Post*, June 25, 2018, https://nypost.com/2018/06/25/video-game-addiction-ruined-my-life/.
3. Andrew P. Doan with Brooke Strickland, *Hooked on Games: The Lure and Cost of Video Game and Internet Addiction* (Coralville, IA: F.E.P. International, 2012), 18.
4. "Empathy: College Students Don't Have as Much as They Used To," University of Michigan, May 27, 2010, https://news.umich.edu/empathy-college-students-don-t-have-as-much-as-they-used-to/.
5. Sherry Turkle, *Reclaiming Conversation: The Power of Talk in a Digital Age* (New York: Penguin Books, 2015), 6.
6. Josh Burnette (author of *Adulting 101*), in discussion with author, October 18, 2019.

7. Andrew K. Przybylski and Netta Weinstein, "Can You Connect with Me Now? How the Presence of Mobile Communication Technology Influences Face-to-Face Conversation Quality," *Journal of Social and Personal Relationships* 30, no. 3 (2012): 237–46, https://doi.org/10.1177/0265407512453827.
8. "Media and Children Communication Toolkit," American Academy of Pediatrics, https://www.aap.org/en-us/advocacy-and-policy/aap-health-initiatives/Pages/Media-and-Children.aspx.
9. Katherine Nelson, "Structure and Strategy in Learning to Talk," *Monographs of the Society for Research in Child Development* 38, no. 1/2 (February to April 1973): 1–135, http://doi.org/10.2307/1165788; Deborah Linebarger and Dale Walker, "Infants' and Toddlers' Television Viewing and Language Outcomes," *American Behavioral Scientist* 48, no. 5 (January 2005): 624–45, https://doi.org/10.1177/0002764204271505.
10. "The Common Sense Census: Media Use by Kids Age Zero to Eight," Common Sense Media, 2017, https://www.commonsensemedia.org/sites/default/files/uploads/research/0-8_executivesummary_release_final_1.pdf, 18.
11. Marie Evans Schmidt et al., "The Effects of Background Television on the Toy Play Behavior of Very Young Children," *Child Development* 79, no. 4 (2008): 1137–51, https://www.doi.org/10.1111/j.1467-8624.2008.01180.x.
12. Victoria Rideout et al., "The Media Family: Electronic Media in the Lives of Infants, Toddlers, Preschoolers and Their Parents," Henry J. Kaiser Family Foundation, May 2006, https://www.kff.org/wp-content/uploads/2013/01/7500.pdf.
13. Kayt Sukel, "The Truth about Research on Screen Time," Dana Foundation, November 6, 2017, https://dana.org/article/the-truth-about-research-on-screen-time/.

Chapter 3: Screen Time and Safety

1. "The Common Sense Census: Media Use by Tweens and Teens," Common Sense Media, 2019, https://www.commonsensemedia.org/sites/default/files/uploads/research/2019-census-8-to-18-full-report-updated.pdf, 3.
2. Aaron Smith, Skye Toor, and Patrick Van Kessel, "Many Turn to YouTube for Children's Content, News, How-To Lessons," Pew Research Center,

November 7, 2018, https://www.pewinternet.org/2018/11/07/many-turn-to-youtube-for-childrens-content-news-how-to-lessons/.

3. Josephine Bila, "YouTube's Dark Side Could Be Affecting Your Child's Mental Health," CNBC, February 13, 2018, https://www.cnbc.com/2018/02/13/youtube-is-causing-stress-and-sexualization-in-young-children.html.
4. Meg Meeker, "Helping Your Daughter Become a Confident Woman (Part 2)," Focus on the Family, December 6, 2019, https://www.focusonthefamily.com/episodes/broadcast/helping-your-daughter-become-a-confident-woman-part-2-of-2/.
5. "Internet Statistics," Guard Child, accessed September 12, 2019, https://www.guardchild.com/statistics/.
6. Sheri Madigan et al., "Prevalence of Multiple Forms of Sexting Behavior Among Youth: A Systematic Review and Meta-analysis," *JAMA Pediatrics* 172, no. 4 (2018): 327–35, https://jamanetwork.com/journals/jamapediatrics/fullarticle/2673719.
7. "Prevalence of Multiple Forms of Sexting Behavior Among Youth: A Systematic Review and Meta-analysis," *JAMA Pediatrics* 172, no. 4 (2018): 327–35.
8. Sloane Ryan, "I'm a 37-Year-Old Mom & I Spent Seven Days Online as an 11-Year-Old Girl. Here's What I Learned.," Medium, December 13, 2019, https://medium.com/@sloane_ryan/im-a-37-year-old-mom-i-spent-seven-days-online-as-an-11-year-old-girl-here-s-what-i-learned-9825e81c8e7d.
9. Joanna Stern, "iPhone Privacy Is Broken . . . and Apps Are to Blame," *Wall Street Journal*, May 31, 2019, https://www.wsj.com/articles/iphone-privacy-is-brokenand-apps-are-to-blame-11559316401?mod=searchresults&page=3&pos=5.
10. Britney Fitzgerald, "Facebook Age Requirement: Children Lying About How Old They Are May Put Peers at Risk," *HuffPost*, November 30, 2012, http://www.huffingtonpost.com/2012/11/30/facebook-age-requirement-lying-study_n_2213125.html.
11. "Cell Phone Radio Frequency Radiation," National Toxicology Program, accessed December 9, 2019, https://ntp.niehs.nih.gov/whatwestudy/topics/cellphones/index.html.
12. Pei-Chang Wu et al., "Epidemiology of Myopia," *Asia Pacific Journal of*

Ophthalmology 5, no.6 (November/December 2016): 386–93, www.doi.org/10.1097/APO.0000000000000236.

13. Advent Health, "Generation Deaf: Millennials and Earbud-Induced Hearing Loss," AdventHealth Orlando, June 8, 2016, https://www.adventhealth.com/hospital/adventhealth-orlando/blog/generation-deaf-millennials-and-earbud-induced-hearing-loss.
14. Kathryn Nathanson and Susan Donaldson James, "Generation Deaf: Doctors Warn of Dangers of Ear Buds," NBC News, May 17, 2015, https://www.nbcnews.com/health/health-news/generation-deaf-doctors-warn-dangers-ear-buds-n360041.
15. Lindsay Bever, "'Text Neck' Is Becoming an 'Epidemic' and Could Wreck Your Spine," *Washington Post*, November 20, 2014, https://www.washingtonpost.com/news/morning-mix/wp/2014/11/20/text-neck-is-becoming-an-epidemic-and-could-wreck-your-spine/.
16. Meera Senthilingam, "One-third of world now overweight, with US leading the way," *CNN*, June 12, 2017, https://www.cnn.com/2017/06/12/health/global-obesity-study/index.html.
17. Thomas N. Robinson et al., "Screen Media Exposure and Obesity in Children and Adolescents," *Pediatrics* 140 (November 2017): S97–S101, www.doi.org/10.1542/peds.2016-1758K.

Chapter 4: Screen Time and Emotional Health

Epigraph: Henry Cloud, "Don't Wait for God to Bring You a Date," interview by Beliefnet, March 2005, https://www.beliefnet.com/love-family/relationships/2005/03/dont-wait-for-god-to-bring-you-a-date.aspx.

1. Justin Patchin, "New National Bullying and Cyberbullying Data," Cyberbullying Research Center, October 10, 2016, https://cyberbullying.org/new-national-bullying-cyberbullying-data.
2. "Prevent Cyberbullying," StopBullying.gov, accessed October 2, 2019, https://www.stopbullying.gov/cyberbullying/prevention/index.html.
3. Melanie Hempe, *The Screen Strong Solution: How to Free Your Child from Addictive Screen Habits* (Matthews, NC: Families Managing Media, 2019), 9.
4. "Depression on the Rise Among Teens, Especially Girls, Johns Hopkins Study Finds," Johns Hopkins University, November 16, 2016, https://hub.jhu .edu/2016/11/16/adolescent-depression-study/.

5. Amy Ellis Nutt, "Why Kids and Teens May Face Far More Anxiety These Days," *Washington Post*, May 10, 2018, https://www.washingtonpost.com/news/to-your-health/wp/2018/05/10/why-kids-and-teens-may-face-far-more-anxiety-these-days/.
6. Quentin Fottrell, "Nearly Half of Americans Report Feeling Alone," MarketWatch, October 10, 2018, https://www.marketwatch.com/story/america-has-a-big-loneliness-problem-2018-05-02.
7. Jean M. Twenge, "Have Smartphones Destroyed a Generation?," *Atlantic*, September 2017, https://www.theatlantic.com/magazine/archive/2017/09/has-the-smartphone-destroyed-a-generation/534198/?utm_source=twb.
8. Hugues Sampasa-Kanyinga and Rosamund Lewis, "Frequent Use of Social Networking Sites Is Associated with Poor Psychological Functioning Among Children and Adolescents," *Cyberpsychology, Behavior, and Social Networking* 18, no. 7 (July, 2015), https://doi.org/10.1089/cyber.2015.0055.
9. "Identifying Signs of Stress in Your Children and Teens," American Psychological Association, accessed August 10, 2019, https://www.apa.org/helpcenter/stress-children.
10. Kay Warren, "National Day of Prayer for Faith, Hope, and Life," *Kay's Blog*, August 30, 2017, http://kaywarren.com/kays-blog/national-day-of-prayer-for-faith-hope-and-life/.
11. "Mental Health by the Numbers," National Alliance on Mental Illness, accessed September 20, 2019, https://www.nami.org/Learn-More/Mental-Health-By-the-Numbers.
12. Morning Edition, "CDC Finds Rising Suicide Rates for Young People," NPR, October 17, 2019, https://www.npr.org/2019/10/17/770848694/cdc-finds-rising-suicide-rates-for-young-people.
13. Henry Cloud, "Don't Wait for God to Bring You a Date," interview by Beliefnet, March 2005, https://www.beliefnet.com/love-family/relationships/2005/03/dont-wait-for-god-to-bring-you-a-date.aspx.
14. Marla Eisenberg et al., "Correlations between Family Meals and Psychosocial Well-Being among Adolescents," *Archives of Pediatrics and Adolescent Medicine* 158, no. 8 (2004):792–96, www.doi.org/10.1001/archpedi.158.8.792.
15. Sue Shellenbarger, "The Secret Benefits of Retelling Family Stories," *Wall Street Journal*, November 11, 2019, https://www.wsj.com/articles/

the-secret-benefits-of-retelling-family-stories-11573468201?mod=searchresults&page=1&pos=1.

Chapter 5: Screen Time and the Single Parent

Epigraph: Chuck Swindoll, Charles R. Swindoll, *The Swindoll Study Bible*, NLT (Carol Stream, IL: Tyndale, 2017), 1170.

1. "Screen Time and Children: How to Guide Your Child," Mayo Clinic Staff, June 20, 2019, accessed November 22, 2013, http://www.mayoclinic.com/health/children-and-tv/MY00522.

Chapter 6: The A+ Skill of Affection

Epigraph: C. S. Lewis, *The Four Loves* (New York: Harcourt Brace & Company, 1960), 53.

1. Turkle, *Reclaiming Conversation*, 390.
2. Email interview to author, September 4, 2013.

Chapter 7: The A+ Skill of Appreciation

Epigraph: Cicero, quoted in Alex Wood, Stephen Joseph, and Alex Linley, "Gratitude-Parent of all virtues," The British Psychological Society, https://thepsychologist.bps.org.uk/volume-20/edition-1/gratitude-parent-all-virtues.

1. Kristen Welch, *Raising Grateful Kids in an Entitled World* (Carol Stream, IL: Tyndale, 2015), 17.
2. Emily Campbell, "Grateful Schools, Happy Schools," *Greater Good Magazine*, November 18, 2013, https://greatergood.berkeley.edu/article/item/grateful_schools_happy_schools.
3. Jessica Stillman, "Gratitude Physically Changes Your Brain, New Study Says," *Inc.*, January 15, 2016, https://www.inc.com/jessica-stillman/the-amazing-way-gratitude-rewires-your-brain-for-happiness.html.
4. Hanady Kader, "The Science of Gratitude and How Kids Learn to Express It," Seattle Children's Hospital, November 23, 2015, https://pulse.seattlechildrens.org/the-science-of-gratitude-and-how-kids-learn-to-express-it/.
5. Tom Ziglar, "The Gratitude Journey," Ziglar Foundation, https://www.ziglar.com/articles/the-gratitude-journey/.
6. Shawn Achor, *The Happiness Advantage* (New York: Crown Business, 2010), 7.

7. Jeffrey Froh and Giacomo Bono, "Gratitude in Youth: A Review of Gratitude Interventions and Some Ideas for Applications," *Communique* 39, no. 5 (January-February 2011): 26–28, https://eric.ed.gov/?id=EJ920352.
8. C. Nathan DeWall et al., "A Grateful Heart is a Nonviolent Heart: Cross-Sectional, Experience Sampling, Longitudinal, and Experimental Evidence," *School Psychological and Personality Science* 3, no. 2 (September 2011): 232–40, https://doi.org/10.1177/1948550611416675.
9. 30 Christian Quotes about Thankfulness, Crosswalk, November 14, 2016, https://www.crosswalk.com/faith/spiritual-life/inspiring-quotes/30-christian-quotes-about-thankfulness.html.

Chapter 8: The A+ Skill of Anger Management

Epigraph: Mark Twain, quoted in Tomas Chamorro-Premuzic, "The Upside of Being Angry at Work," *Fast Company*, February 25, 2020, https://www.fastcompany.com/90467448/the-upside-to-being-angry-at-work.
1. Jimmy Kimmel, "YouTube Challenge – I Turned Off the TV During Fortnite," Jimmy Kimmel Live, streamed live on December 13, 2018, YouTube video, https://www.youtube.com/watch?v=QPTXkp4pPeI.
2. Jeff Grabmeier, "'Broad Consensus' That Violent Media Increase Child Aggression," Ohio State University, October 6, 2014, https://www.sciencedaily.com/releases/2014/10/141006142029.htm.
3. Committee of Public Education, "Media Violence," *Pediatrics* 108, no.5 (November 2001): 1222-1226, https://doi.org/10.1542/peds.108.5.1222.
4. Jeannette Nolen, "Bobo doll experiment," Encyclopedia Britannica, accessed November 15, 2019, https://www.britannica.com/event/Bobo-doll-experiment.
5. "Bandura's Observational Theory Influences Violent Behavior through Observation and Imitation Factors," *Applied Social Psychology (ASP)* (blog), Penn State, February 10, 2017, https://sites.psu.edu/aspsy/2017/02/10/banduras-observational-theory-influences-violent-behavior-through-observation-imitation-factors/.
6. Ana Swanson, "Why violence is so contagious," *Washington Post*, December 15, 2015, https://www.washingtonpost.com/news/wonk/wp/2015/12/15/why-violence-is-so-contagious/?noredirect=on.

7. Mike Snider, "Study confirms link between violent video games and physical aggression," *USA Today*, August 8, 2019, https://www.usatoday.com/story/tech/news/2018/10/01/violent-video-games-tie-physical-aggression-confirmed-study/1486188002/.

Chapter 9: The A+ Skill of Apology

1. Gary Chapman and Jennifer Thomas, *When Sorry Isn't Enough: Making Things Right With Those You Love* (Chicago: Northfield, 2013).

Chapter 10: The A+ Skill of Attention

Epigraph: Jerry Seinfeld, "Oprah Talks to Jerry Seinfeld," interview by Oprah Winfrey, from the November 2007 issue of *O, The Oprah Magazine*, https://www.oprah.com/omagazine/oprah-interviews-jerry-seinfeld/all.

1. Michaeleen Doucleff, "A Lost Secret: How to Get Kids to Pay Attention," NPR, June 21, 2018, https://www.npr.org/sections/goatsandsoda/2018/06/21/621752789/a-lost-secret-how-to-get-kids-to-pay-attention.
2. Scott Mautz, "Harvard Study: 47 Percent of the Time You're Doing This 1 (Fixable) Thing That Kills Your Happiness," *Inc.*, May 13, 2019, https://www.inc.com/scott-mautz/harvard-study-47-percent-of-time-youre-doing-this-1-fixable-thing-that-kills-your-happiness.html.
3. William James, *The Principles of Psychology*, vol. 1 (New York: Henry Holt and Company, 1918), 424, http://www.gutenberg.org/files/57628/57628-h/57628-h.htm.
4. Bob Sullivan and Hugh Thompson, "Brain, Interrupted," *New York Times*, May 3, 2013, http://www.nytimes.com/2013/05/05/opinion/sunday/a-focus-on-distraction.html?_r=0.
5. Christine Rosen, "The Myth of Multitasking," *New Atlantis* 20 (Spring 2008): 105–10, http://www.thenewatlantis.com/publications/the-myth-of-multitasking.
6. Ibid.
7. "Data and Statistics about ADHD," Center for Disease Control and Prevention, accessed March 9, 2020, https://www.cdc.gov/ncbddd/adhd/data.html.
8. Kardaras, *Glow Kids*, 123.
9. Chaelin Ra et al., "Association of Digital Media Use with Subsequent Symptoms of Attention-Deficit/Hyperactivity Disorder Among

Adolescents," *JAMA* 320, no. 3 (2018): 255–63, https://jamanetwork.com/journals/jama/article-abstract/2687861.

10. Catherine Steiner-Adair, *The Big Disconnect: Protecting Childhood and Family Relationships in the Digital Age* (New York: HarperCollins, 2013), 123.
11. Kathryn Zickuhr, "In a Digital Age, Parents Value Printed Books for Their Kids," Pew Research Center, May 8, 2013, https://www.pewresearch.org/fact-tank/2013/05/28/in-a-digital-age-parents-value-printed-books-for-their-kids/.
12. Nicholas Carr, *The Shallows: What the Internet Is Doing to Our Brains* (New York: W. W. Norton & Company, 2011), 116.
13. Rutherford Elementary School, accessed October 12, 2013, http://rutherford.jcps.schooldesk.net/.
14. "Want Creative, Curious, Healthier Children with 21st Century Skills? Let Them Play, according to the American Academy of Pediatrics," HealthyChildren.org, August 20, 2018, https://www.healthychildren.org/English/news/Pages/healthier-children-play-according-to-the-AAP.aspx.
15. Carr, *The Shallows*, 219.
16. Rachel Dawkins, "The Importance of Sleep for Kids," Johns Hopkins Medicine, March 12, 2018, https://www.hopkinsallchildrens.org/ACH-News/General-News/The-importance-of-sleep-for-kids.
17. Ibid.

Chapter 11: Screen Time and You

1. Linda Stone, "Continuous Partial Attention," LindaStone.net, https://lindastone.net/about/continuous-partial-attention/.
2. "Kids Resent Parents Who Are Glued to Their Phones, Study Finds," Advocate Aurora Health, accessed December 2, 2019, https://www.ahchealthenews.com/2015/09/29/kids-resent-parents-who-are-glued-to-their-phones/.
3. "Technoreference?," Positive Parenting, January 24, 2018, https://www.childtrends .org/videos/technoference.
4. Adrian F. Ward et al., "Brain Drain: The Mere Presence of One's Own Smartphone Reduces Available Cognitive Capacity," *Journal of the Association for Consumer Research* 2, no. 2 (April 2017): 140–54, https://www.journals.uchicago.edu/doi/10.1086/691462.
5. Beth Kassab, "Are You Addicted to Your Smartphone?," *Orlando Sentinel*, November 25, 2013, http://articles.orlandosentinel.com/2013-11-25/

news/os-disconnect-smartphones-beth-kassab-20131125_1_internet-addiction-smartphone-greenfield.

6. "Mobile Fact Sheet," Pew Research Center, June 12, 2019, https://www.pewinternet.org/fact-sheet/mobile/.
7. Ibid.
8. Andrew Perrin and Madhu Kumar, "About three-in-ten U.S. adults say they are 'almost constantly' online," Pew Research Center, July 25, 2019, https://www.pewresearch.org/fact-tank/2019/07/25/americans-going-online-almost-constantly/.
9. Monica Anderson, "More Americans using smartphones for getting directions, streaming TV," Pew Research Center, January 29, 2016, https://www.pewresearch.org/fact-tank/2016/01/29/us-smartphone-use/.
10. Monica Anderson, "Mobile Technology and Home Broadband 2019," Pew Research Center, June 13, 2019, https://www.pewinternet.org/2019/06/13/mobile-technology-and-home-broadband-2019/.
11. "Despite Clear Benefits, 54% of Smartphone Owners Say Their Phone is 'Not Always Needed'—but 46% Say it is Something They 'Couldn't Live Without,'" Pew Research Center, March 31, 2015, https://www.pewinternet.org/2015/04/01/us-smartphone-use-in-2015/pi_2015-04-01_smartphones_04/.
12. James Fallows, "Linda Stone on Maintaining Focus in a Maddeningly Distractive World," *Atlantic*, May 23, 2013, http://www.theatlantic.com/national/archive/2013/05/linda-stone-on-maintaining-focus-in-a-maddeningly-distractive-world/276201/.
13. "Tributes to Prof," Dallas Theological Seminary, accessed November 20, 2013, http://www.dts.edu/howard-hendricks-tribute/.
14. Dan Ariely, "Ask Ariely: On Pointless Gaming, Topics and Teachers, and Getting Over It," *Dan Ariely* (blog), November, 23, 2013, http://danariely.com/2013/11/23/ask-ariely-on-pointless-gaming-topics-and-teachers-and-getting-over-it/.
15. Cal Newport, *Digital Minimalism: Choosing a Focused Life in a Noisy World* (New York: Portfolio/Penguin, 2019), 28.

Chapter 12: Top Ten Questions and Answers

1. Melanie Hempe, *The Screen Strong Solution: How to Free Your Child from Addictive Screen Habits* (Matthews, NC: Families Managing Media, 2019), 58.

2. Email interview to author, December 17, 2019.
3. Sean Coughlan, "Computers 'do not improve' pupil results, says OECD," *BBC*, September 15, 2015, https://www.bbc.com/news/business-34174796.
4. "Want Kids to Use Tech Productively? That's 'Asking the Impossible,'" Education Week Teacher, October 16, 2018, http://blogs.edweek.org/teachers/teaching_ahead/2018/10/want_kids_to_use_tech_productively_thats_asking_the_impossible.html?cmp=SOC-EDIT-TW.
5. Ferris Jabr, "The Reading Brain in the Digital Age: The Science of Paper versus Screens," *Scientific American*, April 11, 2013, https://www.scientificamerican.com/article/reading-paper-screens/.

Quiz: Is Your Child Addicted to Video Games?

1. Based on Melanie Hempe, "The Video Game Addiction Test," Screen Strong, May 21, 2020, https://screenstrong.com/video-game-addiction-test/.

About the Authors

Gary Chapman has a passion for helping people form lasting relationships. He is the bestselling author of The 5 Love Languages® series and director of Marriage and Family Life Consultants, Inc. Gary travels the world presenting seminars, and his radio program airs on more than four hundred stations. He and his wife, Karolyn, live in North Carolina. For more information, visit his website at 5lovelanguages.com.

Arlene Pellicane is a speaker and author of several books, including *Parents Rising, 31 Days to a Happy Husband,* and *Calm, Cool, and Connected: 5 Digital Habits for a More Balanced Life.* Arlene has been a featured guest on the *Today Show, Fox & Friends, Focus on the Family,* and *FamilyLife Today,* and serves as the host of *The Happy Home* podcast. She lives in San Diego with her husband, James, and their three children. To learn more and get free family resources, visit www.ArlenePellicane.com.

MORE PARENTING RESOURCES

Things I Wish I'd Known Before We Became Parents has one goal: prepare young and expectant parents for the joys and challenges of raising kids. With professional insight and advice from personal experience, Drs. Gary Chapman and Shannon Warden walk you through the ins and outs of rearing young children.

978-0-8024-1474-8

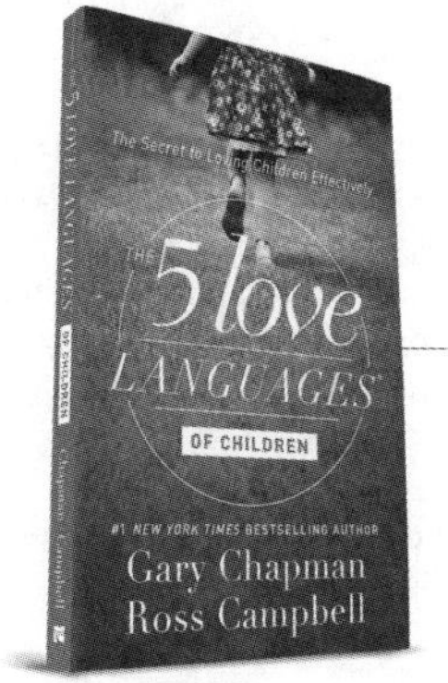

Two family relationships experts help you discover your child's primary love language and how to speak it. Once you learn how to convey love, affection, and commitment in ways that resonate specifically with your child, you will see so much improve, including your child's emotions, behavior, confidence, and relationship with you.

978-0-8024-1285-0

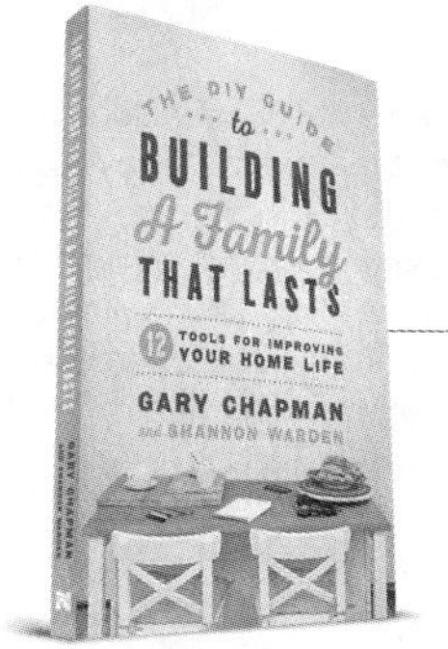

Learn practical tools for transforming your home life and dramatically improving your family's culture from Shannon Warden and Dr. Gary Chapman. Each chapter pairs a home life skill with a home improvement metaphor to make building your family fun and easy to remember.

978-0-8024-1914-9

Also available as eBooks

NORTHFIELD
PUBLISHING

RESOURCES TO STRENGTHEN YOUR MARRIAGE

The COVID-19 pandemic has unexpectedly placed couples in unprecedented proximity. Whether sheltering in place together has been challenging or delightful for you and your spouse, let this time be an opportunity to renew your love. Learn how to do so in *5 Simple Ways to Strengthen Your Marriage . . . When You're Stuck at Home Together.*

978-0-8024-2332-0

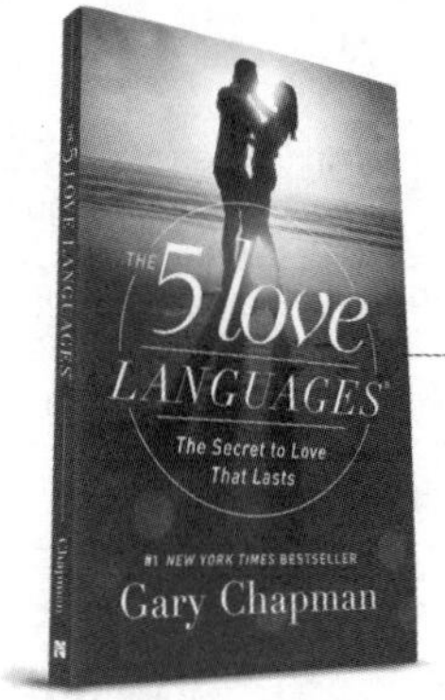

Discover the secret that has transformed millions of relationships worldwide. Whether your relationship is flourishing or failing, Dr. Gary Chapman's proven approach to showing and receiving love will help you experience deeper and richer levels of intimacy with your partner—starting today.

978-0-8024-1270-6

Whether fractured by a major incident or a minor irritation, the emotions provoked can often feel insurmountable, preventing a relationship from moving forward and the offended from moving on. Discover why certain apologies clear the path for emotional healing, reconciliation, and freedom, while others fall desperately short.

978-0-8024-0704-7

Also available as eBooks

NORTHFIELD PUBLISHING